A Scientist Researches
Mary
Mother of All Nations

A Scientist Researches
Mary
Mother of All Nations

By Professor Courtenay Bartholomew

PUBLISHING COMPANY
P.O. Box 220 • Goleta, CA 93116
(800) 647-9882 • (805) 692-0043 • Fax: (805) 967-5843

Dedication

This book is dedicated to Her Majesty,
the Queen of Heaven and Earth.

It is written especially for those Catholics who do not know their faith as well as they should, and for those many Protestants who do not understand the true role of Mary in salvation history.

Library of Congress Number # 99-76003

Published by:
Queenship Publishing
P.O. Box 202
Goleta, CA 93116
(800) 647-9882 • (805) 692-0043 • Fax: (805) 967-5843

Printed in the United States of America

ISBN: 1-57918-123-6

BISHOP'S HOUSE

Morne Jaioux
P.O. Box 375
St. George's, Grenada, West Indies

IMPRIMATUR:
Bishop Sydney A. Charles
St. George's
Grenada
27 July 1999

This is the third work of Professor
Courtenay Bartholomew. It brings
out in a remarkable manner not only
his scholarship, but also the
painstaking and loving care with
which his research was carried out
on the Mother of All Nations, Mary,
Co-Redemptrix, Mediatrix and Advocate, in subordination to her Son,
Jesus Christ, her Lord and God.

Acknowledgements

I wish to express my appreciation to Fr. Paul Sigl for inviting me to assist in the spread of the devotion to the Lady, Mary, Mother of all Nations and the propagation of her prayer and image, and to Dr. Mark Miravalle and the Vox Populi Mariae Mediatrici Movement for involving me in the fostering of an understanding of the doctrinal role of Our Lady as Co-redemptrix, Mediatrix, and Advocate.

I also wish to thank Miss Sharon Baynes and Miss Patricia Virgil for assisting in typing this manuscript, and Ms. Mary Pinder and Sir Ellis Clarke for reviewing the text.

Few understand as deeply as Prof. Courtenay Bartholomew the universal, unique and decisive importance of the Messages of Amsterdam in regard to the final, greatest and most important Marian dogma, through which God will grant true peace and a "New Pentecost of Love" to the Church and the world.

According to the words of the Mother of All Nations, however, the worldwide spreading of the image and prayer which she has revealed, must precede the proclamation of this crowning dogma as direct preparation. In a very original way the author has succeeded to portray Mary in a broad biblical-historical context as "The Lady, Mother of All Nations" in the climax of her vocation.

Those who have had the pleasure of attending on of Prof. Bartholomew's talks will surely enjoy reading his books. This, his most recent work is undoubtedly his most beautiful and interesting yet. He should truly be thanked for this!

— Fr. Paul Maria Sigl
Family of Mary Co-Redemptrix

Contents

Introduction

On May 31, 1996, Bishop Hendrik Bomers, Bishop of Haarlem, Holland, finally approved the devotion to the Blessed Virgin Mary under the title *Mother of all Nations.* It all began in 1945 when Ida Peerdeman, a Dutch visionary living in Amsterdam, claimed to be receiving messages from the Virgin. The series of apparitions frequently occurred on Marian feast days. On February 11, 1951, the feast day which celebrates the date when she first appeared in Lourdes in 1858, the Blessed Virgin said to Ida: "I am the *Lady, Mary, Mother of all Nations.* You may say the *Lady of all Nations* or *Mother of all Nations.* I come on this very day to tell you that I wish to be known as this. Eventually the children of the men of all nations will one day be *one."*

The name Mary in the Hebrew Old Testament is Myriam, Maryam in the Aramaic, Mariam in the Greek translation of the Old Testament, and Maria in the Greek New Testament. Now, there are many suggested meanings of the name Mary. However, St. Jerome proposed a meaning of Maryam based on the Aramaic "mar" which means "lord." According to *Cruden's Complete Concordance to the Old and New Testaments,* the word "lord" means one with power and authority, a master and ruler. In other words, a sovereign. Yahweh is represented in the Old Testament by "Lord." The word is also used for Jesus Christ. The feminine gender became the usual title applied to Mary. It means "Lady." This interpretation enjoyed wide acceptance and became the usual title applied to her in modern languages: for example, My Lady (*Madonna*) in Italian and Our Lady *(Notre Dame)* in French.

On the other hand, in Old English, "Lady" meant "Queen" and was the title of the consort of the king. It was also the female designation corresponding to "Lord" and is used for a woman who rules over her subjects. Even in present-day England the consort of a Lord in the House of Lords is called Lady. The word "lady" also has a hierarchical meaning in the Bible. For example, in Isaiah's lament for Babylon, it is written: "Sit in silence and creep into the shadows, daughter of the Chaldeans, for you would no longer be called sovereign lady of the kingdoms" (Isaiah 47:4-5). However, while the corresponding masculine term "lord" has retained its original and restricted importance, in modern usage its counterpart "lady" is often used as a recognized feminine analogue of "gentleman," and is applied to all women above a loosely defined and variable state of social position. It also means "a refined woman."

The term "Our Lady" should therefore not be interpreted solely as an expression connoting gentility, refinement and graciousness. It is the female equivalent of "Lord." It is a designation of authority and sovereignty. In other words, Mary is the "First Lady" of heaven and earth — but she is also gentle, refined and gracious! And so, she said to Ida: *I am the Lady, Mary, Mother of all Nations.* She later requested that the doctrines of the Church, which had long identified her as the *Co-Redemptrix, Mediatrix and Advocate,* be proclaimed dogma.

Now, since the dawn of history, the fortunes of individual nations have ebbed and flowed like the ocean tides. Some, at the short-lived height of their power, have made their mark on the world and then drifted into obscurity, if not extinction. The Old Testament records the history of a small but significant group of people who grew from a wandering tribe into an established nation which still exists today. In fact, the word "nation" is mentioned more than 350 times in the Bible, and this also brought about my added attention to the biblical importance of the title *Mother of all Nations.*

The Old Testament story of the Jewish nation — and hence the story of Christianity — begins with an itinerant herdsman called Abram. After God called upon Abram and gave him the promise that he was to be the ancestor of a great nation in return for sole worship to him and not to pagan gods, Abram's name was changed to Abraham, which meant "Father of nations," and Sarai his wife was changed to Sarah, meaning "Princess." God then said to Abraham: "I will bless her, and she shall be a *mother of nations*" (Genesis 17:16).

But that Old Testament battle between the woman and her seed and the serpent and his seed, which was started in the Garden of Eden (Genesis 3:15), is still continuing to this day, and there are many theologians and lay faithful who believe that we are in one of the closing phases of that war. Many however seem to forget, or at times not believe, that, like radiowaves and ultramagnetic waves, there are invisible forces around us and that "our wrestling is not against flesh and blood: but against principalities and powers, against rulers of the world of darkness, against spirits of wicked-ness in the high places" (Ephesians 6:12). They are the fallen an-gels who entice us to sin and to reject God, unfortunately, often with much success.

Indeed, although not as yet approved by the Church, but nei-ther disapproved, it is recorded that the Blessed Virgin once said in Medjugorje in Yugoslavia that the sin of today's world is worse than at the time of Noah. In fact, we in this century have also wit-nessed the greatest wars in world history; men killing men, and now in this decade, children killing children. In this and in many other ways the signs of the times appear to be very clear to some, albeit not to others. So it was in the time of Noah. It was a time of violence (Genesis 6:11), and, as the Bible says, they were eating, drinking, and taking wives and husbands when the flood suddenly came (Matthew 24:38). Perhaps it will also be so with "the fire next time" (2 Peter 3:7).

There is, of course, an overtendency on the part of some people to predict the end of time, and in fact there were many such predic-tions in the past, especially towards the end of the first millenium. There are also many such predictions now that we are close to the end of the second millenium. However, whenever I speak of the "end times," I personally do not mean the end of the world. It was not the end of the world when the flood came. I do believe however that there will be a chastisement as never before experienced, if men do not convert. So also did the Blessed Virgin say in Fatima in 1917, Garabandal in 1960, and Akita in 1973.

I have in this book attempted to summarize some aspects of the Old Testament very briefly, so that it could be easily appreciated and readily linked to the New Testament. As St. Augustine of Hippo once said: "While the New Testament lies hidden in the Old, the latter is revealed in the New." In fact, he was so impressed by the way in which the Old Testament foreshadowed Christ that he compared it to a mother in labour and said that it was "pregnant with Christ." I will show how it is also "pregnant with Mary."

I have also attempted to show in scientific terms how today's science is not in conflict with the creation story. Indeed, science has never been. It simply took the twentieth century's advancement in science to open doors which were closed to our limited and sometimes arrogant scientific minds, but which are now open, so open indeed that with the Hubble telescope we can now see far beyond our limited imagination. But even the Hubble is extremely limited!

In my research on Marian apparitions over the years, I have come to consider that, next to Fatima, the apparitions in Amsterdam and the recently approved devotion to and veneration of Mary as *Mother of all Nations* are most important for this latter part of the century. I have researched in depth the meaning and rationale for this title. Briefly, it began with Eve, which means *"mother of the living,"* yet she brought death to mankind. It then followed with Sarah, who, as I said, was first called by God the *"mother of nations,"* and was the matriarch of all the Semitic peoples. But she was only an Old Testament herald of Mary. In this respect, there is one significant word which makes all the difference in matriarchal importance between the two. Mary calls herself the *"Mother of all Nations."*

There are other women-heralds of Mary in the Old Testament and I have dedicated a chapter to them. I have also devoted several chapters to the link between Our Lady of Guadalupe of Mexico and the *Mother of all Nations* of Amsterdam. In so doing, I recently visited and researched the original Shrine of Our Lady of Guadalupe in Extremadura, Spain. Indeed, devotion to this image of Our Lady was very popular at the time of Columbus' expedition in search of the Indies. This was the journey which brought Christianity to the New World and determined many of the names of his island discoveries.

The apparitions in Amsterdam also enticed me to research the history of Amsterdam in an attempt to understand the reason the Blessed Virgin chose this city to appear as the Lady, Mary, Mother of all Nations. Eventually the whole mystery of Mary began to fall somewhat into place for me. I stand corrected — not the whole mystery! Only God and the angels can appreciate this. The limited mind of man cannot fully understand the plentitude of graces bestowed upon her. Yet she has been criticized, ridiculed and vilified, and has been a sign of contradiction. It had to be so. Like Son, like mother! Still, it has always been most perplexing to me how so many people show such little appreciation of and respect for this most unique woman in creation history. This *is* the woman whom the Almighty has chosen to be his mother! Is it possible, I ask you, that he who is so perfect would choose to be born out of imperfection? Surely, the logical response to such a question does not call for a professorship or any university education!

Albert Einstein's intellectual feat is probably unparalleled in the history of the human mind. Referring to creation, he once said: "I want to know how God created this world. I am not interested in this or that phenomenon, in the spectrum of this or that element. I want to know his mind, his thought, the rest are details." But Mary was in God's mind and thought even before the creation of the universe. The Book of Genesis says that on the sixth day of creation "God saw all he had made, and indeed it was very good" (Genesis 1:14-19). But this was not a superlative score which God gave himself. It was *very good*! Indeed, he could have created an even greater earth and a greater sky, but he could not have created a greater or more perfect mother.

What I am saying is that he must have exhausted his omnipotence in creating her. She was therefore beyond "very good." She was the superlative of superlatives. She was God's masterpiece. And so, she said to Juan Diego in Guadalupe, Mexico, in 1531: "I am the perfect and perpetual Virgin Mary, mother of the true God."

I am not simply being quixotic, although, in a sense, I am. I am merely trying to place myself into the "mind of God" with respect to Mary, as Einstein wanted to do with respect to the science of creation.

This is my third and last book in the series *A Scientist Researches Mary,* and in several ways it is, to me, the most important of all. Among other things, it also attempts to rationalize and clarify the apparent confusion surrounding the title Co-Redemptrix, Mediatrix and Advocate. This latter title, like all the previous Marian dogmas and many of her other titles, will be opposed by some and misunderstood by others. I hope, however, that this book will help many to fully understand that she is truly, as her cousin Elizabeth said, *"the mother of my Lord"* (Luke 1:43), and worthy of honour and praise.

Chapter 1

The Lady, Mary, Mother of All Nations (Part I)

It was towards the end of World War I that the Blessed Virgin Mary appeared in the little village of Fatima in Portugal. "World War I is going to end soon," she said to the visionaries of Fatima in her first apparition to them on May 13, 1917. She continued: "But if men do not convert and stop offending God, another and more terrible war will take place during the reign of Pope Pius XI." Sadly, the conditions were not met, the warning was not heeded, and World War II started during the reign of Pius XI.

On March 25,1945, the feast of the Annunciation, towards the end, this time, of World War II, the Virgin appeared to a Dutch visionary, Ida Peerdeman, in Amsterdam, Holland. She received numerous messages and visions, and also Eucharistic experiences between 1945 and May 31, 1984, which at that time was the feast of the *Queenship of Mary*. I first learnt about these apparitions in Holland in 1990, and when I read the contents of the messages which were alleged to have been given to Ida, I recognized a difference in, shall we say, the character and type of messages given by the Blessed Virgin.

On February 11, 1951, the anniversary of the first day she appeared in Lourdes in 1858 as the Immaculate Conception, she called for the worldwide recitation of her special prayer. It is "a simple but powerful prayer," she said: "Lord Jesus Christ, Son of the Father, send now Your Spirit over the earth. Let the Holy Spirit live in the hearts of all nations, that they may be preserved from degeneration, disaster and war. May the Lady of all Nations, who once was Mary, be our Advocate. Amen." I interpret this request as meaning that Her Majesty is asking this prayer to be, as it were, our "*inter*national anthem."

She went on to say: "The nations, together with the Church, understand well, *together with the Church*, will have to say my prayer. Only the Holy Spirit can make the world *one*, can bring peace between the nations.… This present time is the time of the Holy Spirit. All of you must ask the Holy Spirit to make his truth prevail over the world. The world is not going to be saved by force. The world will be saved by the Spirit.… You must realize why I come as the Lady of all Nations. I come in order to rally all nations in the Spirit, in the Spirit of Truth.… I cannot repeat this often enough to the world. Have recourse to the Holy Spirit now."

She then simplified the theology of her requested dogma: "This is the explanation of the new dogma. As Co-Redemptrix, Mediatrix and Advocate I am standing on the globe in front of the Cross of the Redeemer. By the will of the Father, the Redeemer came on earth. To accomplish this the Father used the Lady. From the Lady the Redeemer received only — I am stressing the word 'only' — flesh and blood, that is to say, his body. From my Lord and Master the Redeemer received his divinity. In this way the Lady became Co-Redemptrix by the will of the Father."

She chose to appear in Amsterdam on the feast of the Annunciation, and to the best of my knowledge, the only other shrine in modern times where she first appeared on that significant feast day was in Betania, Venezuela, in 1976. There is an important link. In Betania she appeared as the *Mother, Reconciler of Peoples and Nations.* This is a title very akin to *Mother of all Nations!*

This feast of the Annunciation in Roman Catholic and Eastern Orthodox liturgy is the commemoration of the greatest event in world history, the incarnation of the Son of God. It was the moment when God left eternity to dwell in time in the womb of a virgin. It was the beginning of the story of redemption and at that instant she became the *Mother of the Redeemer.* And so, it is no coincidence that she chose to appear first in Amsterdam on that feast day, standing in front of the Cross of her Son. It reflected Mary's cooperation and journey with the Redeemer from "the crib to the Cross." It was therefore appropriate that she should choose that day to request her *last* Marian title, *Co-Redemptrix, Mediatrix and Advocate*. As she said in Amsterdam: "Co-Redemptrix I was already at the Annunciation." Therein lies the perfect logic of God!

But she did warn that there would be much conflict before the approval of this title. In fact, it is also a title which, in his pride, envy and hatred of her, Satan would not want to be granted. It would be his greatest humiliation because it would then *officially* confirm and advertise worldwide that she, a mere mortal woman, defeated him (through her "seed"). Unfortunately, he would certainly receive much assistance on earth in that denial! But the dogma *will* be proclaimed in God's time. It is the promise of the *Mother of all Nations*.

Now, as a rule the Church does not approve private apparitions at least until the apparitions have ended and it has also been shown that nothing has been said against Holy Scripture and the teaching of the Church. So it was in Amsterdam. In fact, I believe that it would be imprudent of any Catholic to disregard and dismiss the messages of *approved* private apparitions (or for that matter, even apparitions not as yet approved, but still under investigation by the Church) and thereby thwart God's revelations and plan. It carries with it an onerous and accountable responsibility, particularly on the part of the clergy, who guide the flock.

There have been many apparitions in the Old and New Testaments and they continue to occur to this day. Indeed, Mary herself received a most important apparition. It was Gabriel. In the 20th century, the Church, after extensive and painstaking enquiry, eventually approved the apparitions in Beauraing and Banneux in Belgium which occurred in 1932-1933, and in Fatima in 1917. With respect to the latter, Pope John Paul II, in his book *Crossing The Threshold Of Hope,* wrote: "Mary appeared to the three children at Fatima in Portugal and spoke to them the words that now, at the end of this century, seem to be close to their fulfillment." And so, the shepherd of the flock has clearly spoken.

The private revelations of Sr. Faustina Kowalska of Poland (1905-1938) and her "Divine Mercy" messages, which were suppressed for years, were only approved decades later by a decree of April 15, 1978. This was influenced by Pope John Paul II when as Archbishop of Cracow, he led an investigation between 1965 and 1967, relating to the life and virtues of Sr. Faustina. Thirty years later, on May 31, 1996, after fifty-one years of patient observation and assessment, Mgr. Hendrik Bomers, Bishop of Haarlem, Amsterdam, and Mgr. Josef Punt, his Auxiliary Bishop, eventually issued an official statement finally approving public veneration of Mary under the title the *Lady or Mother of all Nations.*

On June 17, 1996, less than one month after this long-awaited approval by her bishop, Ida Peerdeman died at the age of 90. Her mission was completed and she was "called home." An Order of nuns called the Sisters of the Family of Mary Co-Redemptrix, who received papal recognition on March 25, 1995, has been in charge of the chapel in Ida's home in Amsterdam since July 31, 1996. They promote the worldwide devotion of the *Lady, Mary, Mother of all Nations.*

His Excellency Mgr. Bomers personally presided over Ida's funeral service, a tribute to his high regard for this exceptional woman. He began his homily with the words: "We have gathered together here as people who have loved, admired, and esteemed Ida Peerdeman.... I am certainly without a doubt that she was absolutely sincere and truthful about her experiences. Her entire life was dedicated to venerating Mary under the title of '*Mother of all Nations'.*"

One year later, Cardinal Alfons Maria Stickler, on the occasion of the First International Day of Prayer in honour of the *Mother of all Nations,* held in Amsterdam on May 31, 1997, said: "On the occasion of this time of grace, I would like to express my personal conviction concerning the messages which began in Amsterdam in 1945. I see them as a valuable gift. While reading the messages of Amsterdam, which were entrusted to a woman without any theological education, I was impressed from the very beginning by their simplicity and profundity."

Bishop Paul Maria Hnilica, the longest surviving bishop in the Roman Catholic Church, also had this to say on that occasion: "Before I begin speaking about the theme of this conference, I would like to thank the Bishop of this diocese, His Excellency Mgr. Bomers and his Auxiliary Bishop, His Excellency Mgr. Punt, for approving in an official decree the veneration of Mary under the title *Mother of all Nations*. As far as the contents of the messages from Amsterdam and the supernatural origin are concerned, they have stated that everyone is free to form their opinion. I personally, along with others such as Cardinal Stickler, do not hesitate to confess openly that I am convinced about the authenticity of the messages."

He continued: "I have a deep esteem for the prophetic contents of the messages and their unique contributions to the understanding of the vocation of Mary as Co-Redemptrix, Mediatrix and Advocate. These three titles are uniquely united for the first time in the messages of Amsterdam. Mary revealed herself in Amsterdam to a very simple woman named Ida Peerdeman. I personally was acquainted with the visionary who died last year. What especially struck me about her was her simplicity and humility, and amid many sufferings, she lived an unbroken obedience to the Church. Ida Peerdeman, through her faithfulness, through the suffering of not being understood and the calumny which she endured for fifty years, contributed to our being able to be here today to honour the *Mother of all Nations*. Pope John Paul II, who knows from personal experience the value of suffering, has called on the Mother of God several times during his Pontificate as 'Co-Redemptrix of the human race.' Indeed, there has never been a negative decision of any kind from Rome regarding Amsterdam."

Speaking on the same occasion, Fr. Paul Maria Sigl made this comment: "In order to carry out with conviction what is requested in the message, one has to be certain that it comes from God and that the prophet is a prophet of God. The Lord does not expect vain credulity from us. Rather he warns us to beware of false prophets. But when the authenticity is proven, we must open ourselves thankfully to the messages, obey like children and fulfill everything exactly as God through Mary gives us to understand. Only seldom in the history of Marian apparitions does one find such fascinating proofs of the authenticity of the messages as here in Amsterdam. Let us cite only one example. On the night between 18–19 February, 1958, the Mother of God announced to the visionary that in the beginning of October (hence in eight months), Pope Pius XII, who at that time was completely healthy, would die. She said: 'This

Holy Father Pope Pius XII will at the beginning of October of this year be taken up to dwell with us. *The Mother of all Nations, the Co-Redemptrix, Mediatrix and Advocate* will lead him to everlasting bliss.' Pope Pius XII died on October 9 at Castelgandolfo."

In fact, not only did she predict the passing away of Pope Pius XII, as Fr. Sigl said, but, five years later, after receiving Communion on May 31, 1963, Ida heard a voice say: "Do not tell anyone before it has happened." Then she heard: "Montini." Pope John XXIII died three days later on June 3, 1963, and Cardinal Giovanni Montini was elected Pope on June 21, 1963. He took the name Paul VI.

Pope Paul VI died fifteen years later, on August 6, 1978. Ida was praying that the Holy Spirit would enlighten the minds of the cardinals in their choice of a new Pope when she heard the voice again: "He who comes from afar would be Peter's successor." This was repeated on October 16, 1978. That night Ida heard over the radio that the Polish Cardinal Wojtila had been elected Pope in the name of Pope John Paul II!

The following year, on May 31, 1979, once more Ida heard: "The Netherlands will be revived through her whom I have sent. Implore the Spirit of Truth. The Holy Father will proclaim her Co-Redemptrix, Mediatrix and Advocate."

The messages of Amsterdam are very unique in the history of Marian apparitions, not only because Mary herself came in these modern times under a new title, but because, in a way somewhat uncharacteristically, she also requested a last Marian dogma: "It is the wish of the Father and the Son to send me into the world in these times as the *Co-Redemptrix, Mediatrix and Advocate*. When the dogma…has been proclaimed the *Mother of all Nations* will give peace, true peace to the world," she said.

On July 17, 1992, I first visited Ida Peerdeman in Amsterdam and spent several hours with her in the chapel wherein lies the original painting of the *Mother of all Nations*. By coincidence (or was it?), it was, as Ida exclaimed to me, the anniversary date of the miracle of the Eucharist which she experienced in 1951. Ever since, and indeed for some time before that, I have been drawn to the messages of the *Mother of all Nations* and have found them to be the most fascinating of all the messages given in all her shrines.

The prophecies, which in the forties and fifties seemed strange and unimaginable, have largely been fulfilled as the decades have rolled by. Indeed, in my book *A Scientist Researches Mary: Mother and Co-Redemptrix,* I have detailed the results of researching several of her "political" prophecies, which came to pass with time. Recently, however, I have gained new insights with respect to the Amsterdam apparitions, including their link to Our Lady of Guadalupe. But the story of the title, *the Lady, Mary, Mother of all Nations,* really begins in the Book of Genesis.

Chapter 2

Creation – Where Science Meets Religion

Among the ancient peoples, only the Hebrews got their cosmology right. Only they believed in an omnipotent God who gave the universe its beginning, and not in a magical, eternal universe that itself gave birth to the gods. When God took the father of the Hebrews, Abraham, out of his tent (see chapter 5) and told him: "Look up to the heaven and count the stars if you are able to count them," he then said to him: "So shall your descendants be" (Genesis15:5-6). To expect any man, especially an elderly, childless man, to believe that he would have such a number of descendants must have indeed taken a superabundance of faith.

But what Abraham saw and was unable to count was only a microcosm of the macrocosm. In fact the number of stars that actually can be seen at any time with the unaided eye is only a little over two thousand, but there are some hundred billion stars in our galaxy alone. As the psalm says: "The heavens declare the glory of God; the skies proclaim the work of his hands" (Psalm 19:1).

The Big Bang theory of the creation of the universe, the most credible so far, enables scientists to understand the biblical account of Genesis in the light of science. At the beginning of the century it was thought that the Milky Way was our only galaxy, however, because of Edwin Hubble's telescope, we now recognize that there are about a hundred billion others, and each has billions of stars, all fleeing away from one another as if they are remnants of a once enormous explosion. Of course, it raises the question of whether there is other life "out there," the answer to which in either direction will be mind-boggling and in one case would raise important theological questions.

The Hubble Law is one of the great discoveries in science and is one of the main supports of the scientific background of Genesis. However, this immensity of the cosmos and the understanding of it is best told in the Bible in God's conversation with Job.

God said to Job:

> *"Where were you when I laid the foundation of the earth? Tell me, if you have understanding. Who determined its measurement — surely you know! ... Who laid the cornerstone when the morning stars sang together and all the heavenly beings shouted for joy? Or shut in the sea with doors when it burst out from the womb? ... Have you comprehended the expanse of the earth? Declare, if you know all this.... Do you know the celestial laws of the heavens? Can you establish these rules on earth?"* (Job 38:4-33).

Indeed, all the scientific laws of the universe are very precise and we know that these laws result in symmetry, harmony, balance, and ultimately in highly developed living forms. Such a finely controlled creation defies both atheism and all the religions of pantheism. However, the origin and size of the cosmos are still beyond human understanding, and lost somewhere between this immeasurable immensity and eternity is our tiny planetary home.

Now, the fundamentalists would say that the age of the universe is exactly the age derived from the generations as they are listed in the Book of Genesis. This comes up to approximately 5,700 years. For them, the cosmological estimate of the age of the universe, which is now thought to be about 15 billion years, is a preposterous fiction and not in keeping with the Bible. According to them, the time between the beginning and the appearance of man is said to be six days, and six days it is!

But Old Testament theology talks in the language of the average man, while current cosmology makes its statements in purely scientific terms. To the literalist there was also no prehistoric man. Adam was the first man and he was formed some 5,700 years ago "from the dust of the earth" (Genesis 2:7). However, in the animal kingdom dinosaurs have been firmly established to have roamed the earth for a hundred million years, becoming extinct some 65 million years ago. Archeologists knew that fact centuries before Steven Spielberg! Peking man made his appearance 1.5 to 2 million years ago and there is also archeological evidence that Neanderthal man lived some 300,000 years ago. Looking at their fossils, it is clear that, except for a shortened forehead, these early hominids had features so similar to modern humans that they would go unnoticed if they walked down Park Avenue.

In fact, the human DNA (deoxyribonucleic acid), our genetic make-up, is 98.5 per cent identical to that of chimpanzees. However, despite their genetic similarities, to even the most dim-sighted observer, chimpanzees and humans differ in very many ways. Does it then mean that chimpanzees are nearly human? Not really. Nearly 75 per cent of human genes have some counterpart in nematodes (millimeter-long soil-dwelling worms) but that does not mean that a worm is three quarters on the way to being human. Clearly there is something about that 1.5 per cent of the genome that makes all the difference; something which gives *Homo sapiens sapiens* the ability to write, read, debate, and sing along with the car radio, and even wear tuxedos!

As Gerald Schroeder, an Israeli physicist, set out to prove in his books *Genesis and the Big Bang* and *The Science of God,* the Bible only picks up the story of creation near the close of human development. But biblical data is not totally at odds with archeology, and scientists find no conflict between the chronology of the biblical calendar and the scientifically established dates for the entire *post*-Adam period, that is, the 57 centuries *since* Adam. There can be no doubt that archeology has confirmed the substantial historicity of the Old Testament just as radioactivity studies have shown that, while we believe the universe is 15 billion years in age, the earth is 4.5 billion years old, which is similar to the age of the sun, moon and various meteorites. Only the early part of the Bible's calendar, which relates to events that *precede* Adam, *appears* to be in contradiction with the results of modern scientific enquiry. As for *pre*-Adam biblical chronology, how are we to stretch six days to encompass 15 billion years? Or the reverse, how do we squeeze 15 billion years into six days?

The first two chapters of Genesis describe the universe's step-by-step formation. For the first one or two days of the six days of Genesis, the earth did not even exist, for although Genesis 1:1 says: "In the beginning God created the heavens and the earth," the very next verse says: "The earth was a formless void." The first verse of Genesis is therefore a general statement meaning that, in the beginning, a primeval substance was created, and from this substance the heavens and the earth would be made during the subsequent six days. This is explicitly stated in Exodus 31:17: "For six days God made the heavens and the earth." Now, as we shall see, Genesis 1:5 says: "Evening came and morning came: the first day." This is the first time that a day is quantified: evening and morning. Does it mean sunset and sunrise? It would certainly seem to. The text goes on to say the same for the second and the third day. Then on the fourth day, the sun is mentioned. How can there be such a concept of evening and morning for the first three days if the sun is only mentioned on the fourth day? And so, "day" in the Bible is not "day" as we know it.

Now, it is today's scientific belief that prior to the creation of the universe, time and space did not exist. Of course, such a condition almost seems to be an impossibility as we cannot visualize total spacelessness and timelessness. However, the creation of the heavens and the earth from absolute nothing is the root of biblical faith. But it took Einstein and his special theory of relativity (1905) and then his general theory of relativity (1906) to teach us about space and time. He also demonstrated two fundamental entities, the nature of light and the existence of atoms. He showed that no matter the motion of its source, light always travels at a constant speed (about 186,000 miles per second). In so doing, he transformed the entire way in which science and our understanding of space and time viewed the world.

Einstein's law, $E=mc^2$, states that energy and mass are actually different states of a single energy-matter continuum. Energy is matter in its intangible form; matter is energy in its tangible form, and both may be converted into each other. According to $E=mc^2$, where E is energy, m is mass and c is the speed of light, matter is solidified energy and if mass could somehow be converted into energy, a tiny amount of mass would release an awesome and tremendous amount of energy. As the speed of light is approximately 186,000 miles per second, we see that one unit of mass will release nearly 35,000,000,000 units of energy (It was this equation which eventually gave birth to a monster. It was called the atomic bomb. But it was not Einstein's intention).

Cosmologists now believe that the presence of the energy and matter of the universe not only caused the existence of time into which it flows, but also of the space into which it expands. It was the result of a so-called Big Bang. It is a theory first proposed in 1946 by George Gamow and his collaborators. It was a massive expansion from that single miniscule core of a fireball. At that instant the substance of the universe received a powerful push. Physicists believe that just after that time the four basic forces of nature — gravitational, electromagnetic, and the strong and weak nuclear forces — were unified.

But to understand fully the equation of Einstein's general theory of relativity requires a level of mathematical knowledge that few of us possess. One story from the 1920s has it that a reporter asked the famed physicist Arthur Eddington, a relativity expert, if it was true that only three people in the world understood Einstein's theory. After a long pause Eddington finally replied: "I was just trying to think who the third person is."

However, to access the universe is essentially to enquire into the atom, as the atomic structure appears to be an intimate and constant part of the matter of our universe. It was not until around 1910 at Cambridge University in England that the nature of the atom was first understood. They are very small and 100,000,000 of them end to end would only be as large as the tip of a finger. But the nucleus is a hundred times smaller still, which is part of the reason it took so long to be discovered by Ernest Rutherford.

Atoms are composed of three kinds of elementary particles — protons, neutrons, and electrons. This "trinity" of units put together in various patterns makes essentially everything. Indeed, we are all made of atoms. The neutrons, as their name suggests, carry no electric charge. The protons have a positive charge and the electrons have an equal negative charge. Electrons are the lightest of the these particles. In short, atoms are made of nuclei and electrons and nuclei are made of protons and neutrons.

Scientists in the field have estimated that the temperatures in the early universe were so high that atoms could not form, but about three minutes after the Big Bang the temperature of the expanding universe had dropped to about one billion degrees. Protons and neutrons could then clump to form atomic nuclei. After about 100,000 years, when the temperature had fallen to 3,000 degrees or so, electrons then bound with the nuclei, creating full-fledged atoms. Hydrogen and helium then appeared. Hydrogen is an atom with a single proton (the nucleus) and one electron. This is the lightest element. Heavier elements are formed by fusion of the lighter elements. For example, helium, the second element by atomic weight, is formed by the fusion of two protons and two neutrons, while uranium has a complex nucleus made up of 92 protons and 146 neutrons.

As the universe expanded, and as temperatures and energies fell further, hydrogen then rapidly fused into deuterium (with one neutron attached to hydrogen) and then into helium, which might then absorb more protons and neutrons, and in doing so build heavier elements like carbon, nitrogen, oxygen and iron.

After several hundred thousand years passed, temperatures and photon energies (the particles of light and other forms of electromagnetic radiation) continued to fall in proportion with the universe's expansion, and when the temperatures fell below 300 degrees Celsius, a critical event occurred. Light separated from matter and emerged from the darkness of the universe. We are, shall we say, prejudiced towards light. It is what we see. But just as there are sounds too high-pitched and too low-pitched for us to hear, so there are also frequencies of light outside our range of vision, e.g. gamma rays, X-rays, radio waves, microwaves and ultraviolet light wavelengths.

And so, although photons (the particles of which light is composed) were and are the main components of the universe, the universe was dark. They were held in a confused soup of random collisions with masses of free electrons. Only after some hundreds of thousands of years, when cosmic temperatures fell to a level that permitted electrons to bind in orbits around atomic nuclei, did the ubiquitous photon-electron collisions cease. Photons were then freed from long bondage with matter and they burst forth, bathing the universe in a blaze of light.

Meanwhile as the earth continued to cool, steam began to rise up from the earth and the volcanic rocks to form the seas. The Bible puts it this way:

> *Now the earth was a formless void, there was darkness over the deep, and God's spirit hovered over the water. God said, 'Let there be light,' and there was light. God saw that light was good, and God divided light from darkness. God called light 'day,' and darkness he called 'night.' Evening came and morning came: the first day* (Genesis 1:3-5).

Now, light and water are the prerequisites for photosynthetic growth of plants, and a by-product of photosynthesis is the release of molecular oxygen. Indeed, the ability of photosynthesis to oxygenate the world is tremendous. On the third day of Genesis, plant life appeared. Early plants produced oxygen which enriched and changed the atmosphere, also building up the protective ozone layer. This allowed for further development of life.

The Bible reads:

> *God also said, 'Let the earth put forth vegetation, plants yielding seeds, and fruit trees bearing fruit.... And God saw that it was good. Evening came and morning came: the third day* (Genesis 1:11-13).

When the matter of the universe was freed from the constant bombardment by photons, matter now consisted of approximately 75 percent hydrogen and 25 percent helium, which in time could begin to cluster and to form galaxies and stars. All the elements necessary for life, carbon, nitrogen, oxygen, iron, iodine, et cetera, and the really heavy elements such as gold and uranium, did not yet exist. It was a universe of hydrogen, helium, photons and neutrinos.

Neutrinos resemble electrons but carry no electric charge, and play no part in the gross structure of matter. In very early times, these neutrinos were coupled to the photons, and although they no longer interact with them, they are still there. They spend their time flying blindly across the cosmos, only rarely, if ever, interacting with any matter they encounter along the way. In fact, in the time you take to read this page some 30 trillion neutrinos will pass through the page leaving no trace of their existence. Even solid rock is no obstacle. They are so numerous that they contribute significantly to the cosmic dark matter, and are the only nonbaryonic dark-matter particle candidate that is known to exist. It is because of the particle's lack of an electric charge that it was later dubbed the "neutrino," the Italian for "little neutral one."

When oases of light appeared in the vast expanse of dark space, with this separation of light from matter, matter could now start to coalesce and form the earth and its satellite planets. The Bible records that stage of creation in its own non-scientific language.

> *God said, 'Let the waters under heaven come together under a single mass.... God called the dry land 'earth' and the mass of waters 'seas.' And God saw it was good....* (Genesis 1:9-10).

Diffuse matter, mainly the nebulous gases of primeval hydrogen and helium, then clustered to form a galaxy of stars. Fusion among the nuclei started the nuclear furnaces, which we call stars, and which still dot our night skies with light. Of course, all these accounts of the scientific processes of creation, grossly oversimplify, to say the least, what was a much more complex evolution.

Eventually from this stellar fusion came, and still come all the elements present in our universe other than hydrogen and helium — carbon, nitrogen, oxygen, iron, et cetera. As a matter of fact, we are all star dust and the human body is composed mainly of oxygen (65%), carbon (18%), hydrogen (10%), nitrogen (3%) and smaller percentages of calcium, potassium, sodium, iron, et cetera.

So said, it was on the fourth day that the two great luminaries appeared in the firmament of heaven (Genesis 1:14).

> *God said, 'Let there be lights in the vaults of heaven to divide day from night.... And so it was. And God made the two great lights: the greater light to govern the day and the smaller light to govern the night; he made the stars.... God saw that it was good. Evening came and the morning came: the fourth day* (Genesis 1:14-19).

At this time, the sun, moon and stars, already visible in the firmament, became visible on earth as individual sources of light. This biblical account was obviously from an earthly viewpoint because the earth is the only celestial body close enough to the moon and the sun to see them as great luminaries.

The Bible then records that animal life appeared in the waters on day five and on the dry earth on day six. This is after the sun became visible in the firmament of heaven on day four. This is logical. It was also the availability of oxygen that allowed the development of life forms larger than bacteria and algae.

It was now day six:

> *God said, 'Let us make man in our own image, in the likeness of our selves.... And so it was. God saw all he had made, and indeed it was very good. Evening came and morning came: the sixth day* (Genesis 1: 14-19).

When on the sixth day God decided to make mankind, the Bible narrative states that God made man in his own image and likeness (Genesis 1:26), and at the end of the description of the making of the universe, Genesis 1:31 states: "And it was very good." In other words, creation had progressed from good to *very* good. It was a change from disorder without a possibility of life to an order with life. The physical course was prepared for its ultimate purpose. The environment for mankind was in place. It was created by the Master Physicist, Mathematician, Architect, Biologist and Chemist. The Garden of Eden was ready and "user-friendly," to use a computer terminology.

However, a special ingredient not mentioned before is summoned at this junction. God "breathed" the soul of life into Adam and man became a special living being, each with his own fingerprint; each with his own DNA!

> *Yahweh God fashioned man of the dust from the soil.*
> *Then he breathed into his nostrils a breath of life, and*
> *thus man became a living being* (Genesis 2:7).

Now, the soul is a spirit, and is called the "breath of God" because it is created by God in its spiritual or breath-like nature (*Radio Replies'* First Volume, Rumble and Carty, 1979). However, mankind and his predecessors, although physically related, are not connected by a spiritual line of evolution. *Homo sapiens* roamed the earth for some 300,000 years in our space-time reference frame prior to the appearance of mankind, but neither the Neanderthals nor the Cro-Magnons evolved into human beings.

At a crucial junction some 5,700 years ago, a quantum change occurred and the name chosen for the first of the species *Homo sapiens sapiens* was Adam. No direct linkage to the hominid predecessors has been discovered. The link is still missing. Into the physical form of Adam the Creator placed a soul. It is this that has set mankind apart from the other animals, and so, perhaps, to be more accurate, modern man should be relabelled *Homo sapiens sapiens spiritus* for he is a spirit-indwelled being. Humans were then made the caretakers of the earth but accountable to the Landlord. In the biblical narrative we see that creation flowed from chaos to cosmos, a flow from disorder towards increasing order in the material of the universe until it was not only good, but *"very"* good. God rested on the seventh day from all the work he had done in creation (Genesis 2:3-1). Indeed, he has not created any additions to the universe since Adam and Eve. In a sense, therefore, we are still in the seventh day (but he is ever creating souls).

When the physical universe was prepared and mankind was in place, from this time forward, there would be an interplay between man's free will and his knowledge of the will of the Creator. He had no choice. Man had to have a free will. As science writer Fred Heeren philosophized: "So what might a super-intelligent, caring

Creator do? Make creatures who have no wills of their own, so that they cannot bring evil into his perfect universe? Not if God desired to have an eternal relationship with the people who would *willingly* return his love. The very idea of a real will to love requires the real possibility of a person's will to reject it.

"So what might be God's options after his race of free-will creatures broke the harmony of his universe? He could exterminate them. He could simply overlook their injustices. He could leave them alone and let them try to straighten out themselves. But none of these options show the forethought of a perfect, super-intelligent, caring Creator. What then did God do? *He died for us*. He showed both perfect justice and unbounded mercy. And by so doing, he gave those who wanted to be reconciled to him the chance to be forever changed, to be eventually made into fit company for him throughout eternity. This was his predestined plan 'before time began.'"

George Smoot, leader of the satellite team that first detected the cosmic "seeds" of the universe, had this to say: "There is no doubt that a parallel exists between the Big Bang as an event and the Christian notion of a creation…. In fact, the Big Bang theory describes a creation event that defies atheism and pantheism, and harmonizes with the Bible. This theory takes us back to a time when, after the first moment of creation, the entire universe consisted of a region a trillionth the size of a proton."

However, this theory still explains nothing about ultimate origins. What was there before the Big Bang? God! What was there before God? God! Chance could not have formed life. There just was not enough time for this to have occurred by chance. As Einstein once said: "God does not play dice," and as Pope Pius XII concluded in 1951: "True science to an ever-increasing degree discovers God as though God was awaiting each closed door to be opened by science."

Indeed, the modern-day scientist must be possessed by a sense of awe and rapturous amazement at the harmony of the natural law of the universe, which reflects an intelligence of such superiority that, compared with it, all else is insignificant. Creation should therefore inspire not only humility (especially in scientists), but gratitude to the Creator who would go to such amazing lengths in order to prepare a place for us. Creation tells us not only how small we are, but how great he is; how great is his power, his wisdom, his perfection, his beauty, his love. But it does not tell us who made God. The only answer we get from him in the Bible is: **"I AM WHO I AM"** (Exodus 3:14).

In December 1968, three astronauts set off on a mission to orbit the moon. In an historic broadcast to the earth on Christmas eve, Major William Anders was heard reading from the Book of Genesis the passage describing the creation of the world: *"In the beginning, God created the heavens and the earth..."* Then from a quarter of a million miles out in space Captain James Lovel continued: *"And God called the light day and the darkness night..."* Colonel Frank Borman completed the reading with the verse: *"And God said let the waters under the heavens be gathered unto one place and let the dry land appear also."* It was a new dawn for them as they looked down on God's creation.

Chapter 3

The Fall of the Angels

The story of the creation is recorded in the Book of Genesis and brief mention is made of the fall of the angels in several passages in the Old and New Testaments. The Sacred Scriptures also speak of the fall of Satan in the fourteenth chapter of Isaiah:

> *"How did you come to fall from the heavens, Daystar, son of Dawn? How did you come to be thrown to the ground, you who enslaved the nations? You who used to think to yourself, 'I will climb up to the heavens; and higher than the stars of God I will set my throne. I will sit on the Mount of Assembly in the recesses of the north. I will climb to the top of thunderclouds, I will rival the Most High. What! Now you have fallen to Sheol, to the very bottom of the abyss!"* (Isaiah 14:12-15).

The Mystical City of God by the Venerable Maria de Jesus of Agreda (1602-1665) is a monumental four-volume history of the life of the Blessed Virgin, as privately revealed by the Blessed Virgin herself to this seventeenth century Spanish Franciscan nun. It is said that this holy nun saw in ecstasy all the events recorded in her book. The Blessed Virgin told her to write them down, and the book, acclaimed by popes, cardinals and theologians, has inspired the laity and the clergy for over three hundred years. The mystic relates in great detail the account of the creation of the universe and the role of Mary as predestined by God.

She said in Book 1, Chapter 1, that in the beginning God created heaven and earth. He created heaven for angels and men, and the earth as a place of pilgrimage for mortals. The angels were created in the empyrean heavens and in a state of grace by which they might be first to merit the reward of glory. At first, they received a more explicit intelligence of the Being of God, one in substance, three in person, and they were commanded to adore and reverence him as their Creator.

Heaven and earth were hardly created when God dared to reveal his divine plan for the first time, also proposing it as a test for the angelic creatures. The angels were then informed that God was to create a human nature and reasoning creatures lower than themselves, in order that they too should love and reverence him as their Author. They were informed that these were to stand in high favour, and that the second Person of the Blessed Trinity was to become incarnate and assume their nature, raising it to the hypostatic union, and that they were to acknowledge him as their head, not only as God, but as God and man, the God-man, adoring him and reverencing him.

To this command, using their free will, all the obedient and holy angels submitted themselves and they gave their full assent and acknowledgment with a humble and loving subjection of the will. But Lucifer, full of envy and pride, resisted and induced his followers to resist likewise, as they in reality did, preferring to follow him and disobey divine command.

When it was revealed to the angels that they would have to obey the Incarnate Word, a third precept was given to them, namely, that they were to admit as a superior conjointly with him, a woman in whose womb the Only Begotten of the Father was to assume flesh, and that this woman was to be their queen and the queen of all creatures. He then presented her to them, not in reality, since she did not exist as yet, but in a sign or image. It was a woman, adorned with the sun, standing on the moon, and with twelve stars on her head for a crown. St. John describes this image in the Book of Revelation (Rev. 12:1-2). This woman was shown in her condition of motherhood, that is, in a state of maternity. The angelic spirits understood at once the role of this woman.

The mystic went on to relate that the good angels obeyed this latter command of the Lord with still increasing humility, praising the powers and the mysteries of the Most High, accepting also the woman of the sign as their queen. Lucifer and his confederates, however, rose to a higher pitch of pride and boastful insolence. In disorderly fury, he aspired to be himself the head of all the human race and of the angelic orders, and if there was to be a hypostatic union, he demanded that it be consummated in him: "It is only I who will be like the Most High. All will render me honour."

Above all, the decree constituting him inferior to the mother of the Incarnate Word he opposed with horrible blasphemies. Turning against God in unbridled indignation and calling upon the other angels, he exhorted them, saying: "Unjust are these commands and injury is done to my greatness. This human nature which you, Lord, look upon with so much love and which you favour so highly, I will persecute and destroy. To this end I will direct all my power and all my aspirations. And this woman, Mother of the Word, I will hurl from the pedestal on which you have proposed to place her and at my hands, the plan which you set up shall come to naught."

This proud boast aroused the indignation of the Lord and to humiliate and punish him, he spoke thus to Lucifer: "This woman whom you refuse to honour, shall crush your head and by her shall you be vanquished and annihilated. And if through your pride, death enters into the world, life and salvation of mortals shall enter through the humility of this woman. Those that are of the nature and likeness of this man and woman shall enjoy the gifts and the crowns which you and your followers have lost."

Then happened that great battle in heaven which St. John describes in Apocalypse 12. The good angels, led in battle by Michael the Archangel, cast one third of the angelic host down to earth. It was the first warfare in eternity, a war beyond human imagination. It was a disaster unparalleled in eternity and in time. It stemmed from the free will which God in his wisdom had to give his creatures, both angelic and mortal. He had no choice!

In the New Testament, Luke 10:18 records the words of Jesus Himself: *"I watched Satan fall like lightning from heaven."* And so, as Pope John Paul II stated in his encyclical *Redemptoris Mater*, in the mystery of Christ, she is ever present, even before the creation of the world, as the one whom the Father has chosen to be the mother of his Son in the Incarnation.

In the fullness of time, when the earth was hospitable for man, God formed Adam from the dust of the ground and placed him in the Garden of Eden. He then said to him: *"Of all the trees in the garden you may freely eat, but of the tree of the knowledge of good and evil, you shall not eat, for in the day that you eat thereof, you will surely die."* God then caused a deep sleep to fall upon Adam and took one of his ribs and closed up the flesh. One may well say that it was the first biblical record of anaesthesiology and surgery by the Master Surgeon and Physician. A companion was given to Adam. Adam then said: "This one is bone of my bones, and flesh of my flesh. She shall be called woman, because she was taken out of man" (Genesis 2:21-23). He called her Eve, meaning *"mother of all the living"* (Genesis 3:20). This, of course, could also be translated "mother of mankind," or "mother of all peoples."

Now, in this play of life, let us call it Act 3 Scene 1-6 (Genesis 3:1-6) enter the serpent. Satan then tempted Eve first and said to her: "You surely will not die. For God knows that in the day you eat thereof, your eyes will be opened and you will be as gods knowing good and evil." Eve then ate of the fruit and gave it to her husband and he did eat. Satan had his first victory over man. Sin had entered the world — and with it, death.

In Act 3 Scene 15 (Genesis 3:15), God then rebuked the ancient serpent and said to him: *"Because you have done this, I will put enmity between you and the woman, between your seed and her seed. She will crush your head and you will strike at her heel."* It was God's first promise to man that he will redress the situation. Satan knew full well who the woman was. He had previously heard this rebuke when he had seen her in an image form before he fell from heaven!

Chapter 4

The Biblical History of the Nations from Adam to Abraham

Adam and Eve gave birth to Cain and Abel. Out of jealousy Cain killed Abel. It was history's first recorded murder. With the passage of time Cain and his wife gave birth to Enoch. Enoch's son Irad became the father of Mehujael, who in turn became the father of Methushael. Methushael was the father of Lamech. It is written that Lamech married two women and once said to his wives: "Listen to what I say: I killed a man for wounding me, a boy for striking me. Sevenfold vengeance is taken for Cain, but seventy-sevenfold for Lamech" (Genesis 4:17-24). This song of Lamech is recorded as evidence of the increasing ferocity of Cain's descendents.

Adam and Eve went on living for a long time, for people lived for many hundreds of years when the world was new. In time they had many more children and when at last they died, eight hundred years after the birth of one of their sons called Seth, the earth on which they had lived and toiled was a productive land teeming with their children, their children's children, and their great-great-great-grandchildren, who themselves were grown and had children of their own.

It began with Cain and as the centuries rolled by, it seemed that the more people there were on earth, the more wickedness there was upon the earth. Indeed, among them there were only a few who found favour in the eyes of the Lord. These few were descended from Adam's son, Seth. One of them was Enoch. Another was Enoch's son Methuselah, a man who lived longer than any other man in the world. Among his several sons was Lamech, who had a son of his own. That son's name was Noah. He in turn had three sons, Shem, Ham and Japheth.

By that time scarcely any man or woman gave thought to the Lord who had created them. In fact, they became so thoughtless that they no longer knew what was right nor did they seem to care. The earth was corrupt in God's sight and it was filled with violence. Indeed, when the Lord saw that the wickedness of mankind was so great on the earth he was sorry that he had made man. But Noah found favour in the sight of the Lord.

The well-known account of Noah and the ark is recorded in the Book of Genesis, when God destroyed the earth by the great flood of forty days, after which he said to Noah: "I will establish my covenant with you, and with your descendents after you.... There shall be no flood to destroy the earth again. This is the sign of the covenant that I make between me and you and every living creature with you for all generations: I set my bow in the clouds, and it shall be a sign of the covenant between me and the earth. When I gather the clouds over the earth and the bow appears in the clouds, I will remember my covenant between me and you and every living creature of every kind. And so, the waters shall never again become a flood to destroy all things of flesh."

Noah himself lived on for 350 years after the flood. At the age of 950 years, he died, knowing that his sons were to be the fathers of the *nations* of the world. Shem's five sons were to be the fathers of the Semitic people or Hebrews, and from his line would spring two upright men called Abram and Lot. Ham's four sons would go forth and people Africa, and would also be the fathers of the non-Hebrew inhabitants of Canaan. From Japheth's seven sons came the Gentiles or the non-Jewish *nations*. Thus were the families of the sons of Noah separated into the *nations* of the world.

Around 2000 BC, one of the descendents of Shem, a man by the name of Terah, made his home in a great city called Ur in the land of the Babylonians, near the Persian Gulf. Terah had three sons, Abram, Nahor, and Haran. However, many people in those days bowed down to the sun or the moon or the stars, and the people of Ur were such idol worshippers, believing themselves to be especially favoured by the moon god.

When his sons had grown to manhood, Terah, apparently at no one's prompting, decided to leave Ur and go to the land of Canaan, which the people of today call Palestine. He took with him Lot, the son of Haran, Abram and his wife Sarai, his second son Nahor and his wife Milah. However, instead of turning south and going to the land of Canaan, they veered north and settled in the Mesopotamian city of Haran in what is now Turkey. Terah and his family group eventually became the first people in the Bible identified as *Ivriim*, of which the English version is "Hebrews."

The story of Abram and Sarai is recorded in Genesis 12-23. In fact, it is a history that covers more space in the Genesis account than does that of the entire human race from creation down to their time. Such was its importance. When Abram was 75 years old and his wife, "a fair woman to look upon," was 65 years, he heard the voice of the Lord say to him: "Leave your country and your kinsmen and your father's house, and go to a land that I will show you. I will make you a great *nation* and I will bless you and make your name great. Through you shall the families of the earth be blessed." The Lord was referring to Canaan (Palestine).

Abram was obedient to the Lord and willing to forsake home and country for the unknown with Sarai ever at his side. Lot elected to go with Abram, but Nahor and his family decided to remain at Haran. Eventually Abram settled in the land of Canaan and Lot travelled and pitched his tents and pastured his flocks near a city called Sodom. This was about 1850 BC. The city of Ur in Babylonia was a godless place, but Sodom was even worse, as was the neighboring town of Gomorrah.

Now, Abram's wife Sarai was childless and the Lord said to him: "Fear not Abram, I will protect you and reward you greatly for your righteousness." Abram then said to the Lord: "Lord God, what is my reward? I still have no child of my own. Eliezer of Damascus is the steward of my household. Should he be my heir?" "He shall not be your heir; your heir shall be your own flesh and blood," answered the Lord. Then taking him outside, he said to

Abram: "Look up to the heavens and count the stars if you can. Such will be your descendants."

However, throughout the whole of 11 years Abram's wife Sarai still remained childless, and one day, growing impatient for the birth of Abram's promised son, and not understanding the divine delay, she said to Abram: "The Lord has not let me have a child. Go to my handmaid Hagar. Take her to yourself; in that way I may have a child through her." Hagar was an Egyptian maidservant and in those days it was not unusual for a man to have more than one wife, or for a wife to give her handmaid to her husband. And so, childless women like Sarai would sometimes ask their husbands to produce children through a *trusted* handmaid, and the wife would be thought of as the mother of the handmaid's children.

It was not long afterwards that Hagar knew that she was going to have a baby, but she became so proud of it that she began to mock and taunt her mistress who was unable to have a child of her own. When her time came she bore a son to Abram, and they called him Ishmael. However, Sarai could not bring herself to forgive Hagar for her persistent insolence or to accept Ishmael as her own beloved son.

When Abram was 99 years old and Sarai herself, though younger, was past the age when she might have a child, the Lord appeared to Abram again and said: "I am the Almighty God, and I shall make a covenant with you. You have been faithful and have served me well; and you will be the father of many *nations*. From your children, and your children's children, there will come great men and kings, and all the land of Canaan will be theirs forever."

Now, because Abram was to be the father of many *nations*, the Lord told him that his name would change. Instead of being Abram, which meant "exalted father," he became Abraham, which meant "father of a multitude." Sarai, too, must change her name. Her new name would be Sarah, meaning "Princess." "And I will bless her, and she shall be a *mother of nations*...." said the Lord (Genesis 17:16). "I have blessed Ishmael. He, too, will have many children. Twelve princes will descend from him and I will make of him a great *nation*. But my covenant is not with him but with the son of Sarah. For Sarah shall indeed bear a child and you will call him Isaac. I say to you now that Sarah should have a son at this same time next year."

Abraham was 100 years old when a son was born to him and Sarah. They laughed when the Lord said that Sarah would give birth in her old age, but God had the last laugh. He was called Isaac, which means "he laughs." However, because of the continued animosity between Sarah and Hagar, Sarah eventually decided to send Ishmael and his mother away. But God saw Abraham's sorrow and said to him: "Listen to Sarah. Do whatever she says. And do not grieve because of the boy, or because of the woman. It is with Isaac that I have my covenant and it is through Isaac that your name shall be forever known and your family shall be blessed. As for the son of the Egyptian woman, I will also make a *nation* of him, because he is your child. Therefore, have no fear for Ishmael and Hagar."

Eventually God tested the faith of Abraham, the founder of the Hebrew race, from which the Saviour of the world was expected to come: "Abraham, take your son Isaac, your only son, and bring him with you to the land of Moriah. There you will give him up to me as a burnt offering upon a mountain that I will show to you," said the Lord. Even so grieved and heart-broken as he was, Abraham had faith in the Lord and did not question him. The Bible does not detail this but one can also well imagine the extent of the grief of Sarah, she who had waited so long for her first-born.

Abraham took the wood for the burnt offering and laid it on Isaac's shoulder to carry, and father and son went off together to climb the mountain where the offering would be made: "I see the wood and I see the fire, but where is the lamb for the offering?" asked little Isaac. When they came to the place on the top of the mountain that God had told him of, Abraham built an altar of stone and laid the wood upon it. Isaac looked around. He could see no lamb.

Abraham reached gently for his son and tied his hands and feet. This time Isaac asked no question. Then Abraham laid his son upon the wood of the altar and reached out his hand for the knife. He raised it slowly, but when he brought the knife up high, ready for the downward plunge, the angel of the Lord called out to him: "Abraham, Abraham, do not lay your hand upon the boy.

Do not harm him. Now I know that you fear God seeing that you have not withheld your son, your only son, from him." Abraham lifted up his eyes, and behold, behind him was a ram, caught in a thicket by his horn. He gave a name to the place where he was prepared to sacrifice Isaac. He called it Jehovah-jireh, meaning "the Lord will provide."

The Koran, on the other hand, directly contradicts this, and accuses the Hebrew Bible as being fraudulent. Islam states that Abraham had only one son and that Isaac was born afterwards as a reward to him for his obedience to God's command to sacrifice Ishmael. The Koran says that Ishmael was "the son of the promise (covenant)," and not Isaac as the Jews and Christians say. According to the Koran, Ishmael goes to Mecca. His descendents, growing up in Arabia, are Muslims, whereas those of Isaac, who remained in Palestine, are the Jews.

In the New Testament Paul explains the logic of God's favour, and commenting on the birth of Abraham's two sons, he said that Sarah was the free woman who gave birth to a child according to the Spirit while the maidservant Hagar gave birth according to the flesh (Galatians 4:23-31).

Sarah, the first matriarch in the Bible, died when she was 127 years old and Abraham laid his wife to rest in the cave of Machpelah in Hebron. She became the first of all the Hebrew people to die and be buried in the land of Palestine, the land that God had promised the descendants of Abraham. Abraham died when 175 years old and was buried next to Sarah. Today, this *"mother of nations"* still lives on as the woman whose faith helped to achieve the first miraculous birth in biblical history. She was a preherald of the *Mother of all Nations* of the New Testament, Miriam, whom we call Mary.

Chapter 5

The Biblical History of the Nations from Abraham to Jesus

As the years rolled by, Isaac took Rebecca for his wife. Her father was the son of Nahor, Abraham's brother. After Abraham's death, Isaac settled in southern Canaan, and had twin sons, Esau and Jacob. It is written that Jacob, the younger, disguised himself as Esau and thus fraudulently obtained the blessing of his aged blind father. However, in spite of this, Jacob was promised the land of Canaan by the Covenant-God of Abraham and Isaac.

Later, it is related that he spent a night "wrestling with an angel." After that Jacob was called Israel, a name which means "he who strove with God." He married the two daughters of Laban, Leah and later Rachel. The twelve sons he sired were accordingly known as the "children of Israel," and the families they founded thus became the twelve tribes of Israel. His last two sons, Joseph and Benjamin, were mothered by Rachel, who was the first woman to die in childbirth when she was delivering Benjamin.

Now, the favourite of Jacob's (Israel's) twelve sons was his eleventh son Joseph. The Bible relates that his jealous brothers sold him to slavery in Egypt, but his honesty, wisdom and personality eventually earned him the exalted position as Pharaoh's vizier or chief minister. When famine in Canaan drove his brothers to Egypt in search of food, Joseph forgave them, sent for his father also, and obtained land for all of them.

Mannasseh and Ephraim were sons of Joseph and his Egyptian wife, Asenath. Ephraim (then also used as a tribal name) eventually became the most powerful of the twelve tribes and received the choicest land in Canaan. Over the centuries the Hebrews grew greatly in numbers and lived unmolested in Egypt, but sometime after Joseph's death, a new Pharaoh came into power and ordered all the Hebrews to be enslaved. It was in this captivity of over 400 years that the towering figure of the Old Testament arose.

The biblical story says that Moses, the son of Hebrew parents, was hidden in the reeds along the Nile by his mother after Pharaoh had ordered all Hebrew male infants slain. Found and adopted by the daughter of Pharaoh, he was educated at the Egyptian court, but time came when he became angry over the treatment of his people. He killed an Egyptian slave-master, whereupon he had to flee for his life, only to be eventually called by God to redeem the covenant of Abraham and to lead his chosen people back to the Promised Land of Canaan. "Let my people go," Moses then threatened Pharaoh. When Pharaoh refused, Egypt was visited by plagues. However, it was the tenth plague which won the day for the Hebrews. God decreed that a young lamb, without blemish, a one-year-old male, was to be slaughtered and some of its blood daubed on the door posts of the houses of the Hebrews. They were to eat the lamb hurriedly that same night with unleavened bread and bitter herbs for the Lord was to pass through the land of Egypt and strike down each first-born, except those in the households of the Hebrews.

The slaughter took place and Pharaoh finally allowed the slaves to leave and what came to be known as the great Exodus followed. This was between 1250 and 1230 BC. The Red Sea parted and Moses led the Israelites across the Sinai desert until they came to Mount Sinai. At the summit God revealed himself to Moses and gave him the Ten Commandments and the laws of behaviour which became the foundation of the Judaic and subsequently Christian codes. For the rest of their history the Israelites (later the Jews) have regarded the Exodus as their beginning as a *nation*.

God also gave Moses the blueprint for the construction of the Ark of the Covenant to house the two tablets of the Ten Commandments, which in time also contained a ciborium with some of the miraculous manna which fell from heaven to feed the Israelites during their sojourn in the Sinai desert, and later yet, it contained the priestly rod of Aaron, the brother of Moses. This most holy object, the Ark of the Covenant, led the large convoy of Israelites (said to be about 600,000) on their trek to the Promised Land. It was always preceded by the Shekinah, the presence of God. It was a pillar of cloud by day and a pillar of fire by night.

But while Moses received a new order to lead his people back to Canaan and there to create a holy nation, the time had not yet come, nor were the people ready. Moses and his followers wandered around the inhospitable desert for forty years. When 120 years old, Moses again climbed to a mountain summit. This time it was Mount Nebo, and again he heard the voice of God, who showed him from afar the land that he had promised to Abraham, Isaac and Jacob. But for somewhat unclear reasons Moses was himself forbidden to enter Canaan: "This is the land of which I swore to Abraham, to Isaac, and to Jacob. I have let you see it with your eyes, but you shall not cross over there," the Lord said to Moses (Deuteronomy 34:4).

The death of the aged prophet occurred soon after this event. It was then that Joshua, Moses' military lieutenant, took command, led the Israelites across the Jordan River, stormed and captured Jericho, and after many years eventually conquered most of Canaan, which he divided amongst the twelve tribes. As Max Dimont opined in his book *Jews, God, and History,* the biblical account of the destruction by the Jews of the Canaanite culture may sound barbarous to readers unfamiliar with the history and practices of the ancient days. However, the Canaanite civilization fell because the Jews did away with their abominable religious practices — the human sacrifices to the god Moloch, the lewd rites demanded by the Canaanite god known as Baal, and the unrestrained orgies and "sacred prostitution" in the name of a female goddess called Asherah.

Now, after their exodus from Egypt, the people were referred to mostly as Israelites, very seldom as Hebrews. Indeed, the Jews usually referred to themselves as Israelites. When finally, in the twelfth century BC, the "people of Israel" settled in a country they could call their own, they used the worst possible judgement. They selected a piece of land that was a corridor for the armies of warring empires; this little strip of real estate has been alternately called Canaan, Palestine, Israel, Judah, Judea, and now again, Israel.

Years after the settlement of Canaan by the Israelites a distinction was drawn between the people of the North (Israel) and the people of the South (Judah). In their first two centuries in Canaan (about 1200–1025 BC), the loosely confederated tribes of Israelites were ruled by a succession of "judges," who were sometimes military heroes and sometimes judicial officials. All claimed divine inspiration. Among them were Othniel, Ehud, Deborah and Barak, Gideon, Jephthah, and Samson. However, the people of Israel continued to break the covenant and worshiped foreign gods. Enemies continued to press in on them from all sides and the twelve tribes eventually decided to band together and set up a joint monarchy in an effort to resist the expansion of the powerful and well-armed Philistines. It was the beginning of the era of the kings of Israel.

Three kings ruled over all of the kingdom of Israel. They were Saul, David and Solomon. Saul (1030-1010 BC) spent most of his life fighting the Philistines, only to become embittered in his later years by the popularity of a young shepherd named David, who won wide-acclaimed popularity by defeating the Philistine giant, Goliath of Gath. Undoubtedly, the David–Goliath encounter is the Bible's most spectacular duel. First David felled his opponent with a well-aimed shot to his head from a sling, then he decapitated him with the Philistine's own sword.

Saul was subsequently killed in battle with the Philistines and the northern and southern groups of tribes became disunited. When Saul died, David (1010-970 BC) was crowned his successor. It was he who would rid Israel of the Philistine menace and establish a powerful united kingdom over his people. His greatest success was the capture of the "impregnable" city of Jebus, which was to become Jerusalem.

While David extended the kingdom by war, his claim to fame among the Jews rested on other achievements. From the days of

Saul the Ark of the Covenant had been lying in a barn at Kiriath-jearim. David then brought it to Jerusalem and by that act he made it the holy city and political capital of the whole of Israel, where the "portable God" of Sinai would live permanently. However, although David planned to build a temple for the Ark, because he was a warrior king and the temple was dedicated to peace, God did not permit him to build it. This task was entrusted to his son, Solomon. The Lord, on the other hand, would build a house for David, that is, a dynasty. His house and his sovereignty would be everlasting and a descendent of his would forever reign (Psalm 89:3-4).

With David, therefore, God's plan of salvation took a significant step forward. While Abraham was the father of all the Israelites and the one person with whom God initiated the first covenant with the chosen people, and while Moses was the mediator to whom God bound his people in the true covenant-religion at Sinai, David was the king whom God chose to found the kingdom which would be eternal and from which salvation would finally spring through the Mediator of the new and everlasting covenant, Jesus, the Christ, of the bloodline of David.

In fact, the country reached its greatest prosperity and glory under Solomon (970-931 BC), who built the first temple to house the Ark of the Covenant. As one of his biographers wrote: "He exceeded all the kings of the earth for riches and for wisdom." However, he betrayed the moral precepts of his own religion out of his egotistical love of power and splendour, married foreign wives and tolerated their pagan religions.

Solomon reigned for forty years and after his death in 931 BC, his empire was torn apart by internal dissention. Rehoboam, his son, ruled the ten northern tribes in his stead. The two southern tribes under Rehoboam (who reigned for 17 years) retained Jerusalem as their capital and called their kingdom Judah. Indeed, Judah became the guardian of the tradition and was the source of Judaism. The ten tribes in the north, Israel (also referred to as Ephraim), eventually revolted against Rehoboam, and they chose a king of their own for their independent kingdom. He was Jeroboam.

This civil war between Israel and Judah, started by Rehoboam, lasted for as long as a 100 years. However, under Rehoboam's rule, Judah "did evil in the sight of the Lord," building heathen idols and altars on every high hill. Jeroboam in the north, on the other hand, began his reign by deepening the rift between the two countries. He ruled for 22 years and added religious rancor to political acrimony by building a temple in Bethel to rival the one in Jerusalem in the kingdom of Judah. Thus in the eyes of the Lord, there was little to choose between Judah and Israel, the two parts of what was once the Promised Land. Divided, each kingdom became weak and both halves were in danger, not only from their outside enemies, but from each other. Both north and south then sank even deeper into sin, apostasy and degradation.

A succession of inane rulers eventually brought Israel to the brink of chaos from which she was saved by the strong leadership of King Omri (866 BC). But, unwittingly, Omri also laid the foundation for future disaster by marrying his son Ahab to the arch-harlot of history, Jezebel, a Sidonite princess. In fact, so infamous was she that to this day her name is used to describe "a shameless or immoral woman," as the present-day Oxford dictionary states. She fanned the flames of religious hatred and discord by introducing Baal worship, "sacred prostitution," and the sacrifice of children to Moloch, the fire god.

After a reign of 22 years, the death of King Ahab, who was the ruler who broke the covenant more than any other ruler, was a signal for a breakthrough of the pent-up hatred against Jezebel. The conspirators led by the prophet Elisha chose a general named Jehu as king to lead the crusade against the "harlot of Sidon." King Jehu not only assassinated Jezebel but killed every member of the house of Ahab. The worship of Baal was mercilessly exterminated and fifty years of peace and prosperity followed.

However, Israel finally fell to the Assyrian king, Sargon II, in 722 BC. He deported almost the entire population to Assyria, where they were scattered like dry leaves in the wind. Never again did they come together as a nation and never again did they return to the land of their forefathers. They have since been referred as the ten lost tribes of Israel. The kingdom of Israel was over. The history of Judah in the south uncannily paralleled that of Israel in the north and that country's throne was as precarious as Israel's. Twenty kings held it for an average of seventeen years each. Eventually the Babylonians annihilated the Assyrian forces, and when the former Assyrian empire fell into the hands of Babylonia, Judah fell with it.

After a few years of Babylonian rule, Judah staged its first rebellion in 600 BC. However, with King Nebuchadnezzar at the helm of his forces, Jerusalem was besieged and finally fell in 597 BC. Nebuchadnezzar deported 8,000 of the country's leading citizens, all who might possibly foment another uprising. He did not sack Jerusalem at this time or devastate the country. However another anti-Babylonian movement got under way, and in the fateful year of 586 BC, the Babylonians completed the job. The temple was destroyed, the city was looted and reduced to rubble, and everyone was deported to Babylonia, except the poor, the sick and the crippled. However, the Ark of the Covenant was removed from the Holy of Holies in the temple and hidden away by the prophet Jeremiah.

The Babylonians called their captives Jews because they had taken them from Judah and since then they were known as Jews. And so, the kingdom of Judah was finished 136 years after the fall of Israel. Now, when the Babylonians exiled the Jews of Judah, it looked as if this would be the end of them too, but it did not turn out that way. In pagan days, captives marching into exile usually also marched to extinction, not physically, but as a national entity. One set of idols was simply exchanged for another as the captive peoples usually embraced both the idols and the way of life of the conquerors. This was the starting point for assimilation. Indeed, such was the case with the kingdom of Israel. Such, however, was not the case with Judah.

Why then did the Jews of Judah survive whereas the Jews of Israel did not? As Max Dimont put it, it is because the Israelites did not have a conscious will to remain Jews, whereas the captives of Judah carried with them into captivity an implacable will to survive as Jews. The word of their prophets had taken root in their racial, religious, and national memory.

Half a century later, with the defeat of the Babylonians by King Cyrus (600-529 BC), the Jews were flung into the Persian orbit for two centuries. Cyrus then took an action that literally stunned the Jews. He was a humane conqueror and he gave them permission to return to their homeland and rebuild the temple.

Jerusalem became prosperous again. However, many Jews chose to remain where they were instead of going back to Palestine. Then about 300 years later, a Syrian conqueror named Antiochus Epiphanes (175 –167 BC) forbade them to observe the practices of Judaic Law, and desecrated the temple by ordering sacrifices to Greek gods in it. Around 166 BC, a small army of Judah Maccabee, son of an aged Jewish priest, finally drove the Syrians out of Jerusalem and reconsecrated the temple.

When regular services began again in the temple, the *menorah*, the holy candelabrum of seven branches, which has been a holy symbol of Judaism since the time of Moses, and which was a fixture in Solomon's temple, was lighted in this restored temple. Miraculously, it burned for the eight days of celebration on a one-day supply of oil. This miracle of the "Eternal Light" is still celebrated every year during the eight-day Jewish feast of Hanukkah, a festival which serves as an occasion of remembering and thanksgiving.

For the next 100 years the Jews prospered under the Maccabees. Then came the Romans. In 63 BC, Judah became a Roman satellite, which the Romans then called Judea. Years later, in 40 BC, Herod the Great was given the official title of "King of the Jews." Most scholars believe that he was the ruler who ordered the slaughter in Bethlehem of all the Jewish children two years old or less. The Gospel of St. Matthew relates that the decision was prompted by his being told by the wise men of the birth there of a Jewish child whom they called "King of the Jews" (Matthew 2:1-17).

It was 2,000 years after Abraham. Enter Jesus Christ, a descendant of David, son of Jesse of the tribe of Judah. He once said to his disciples: "Do not think that I have come to abolish the law (of the Old Testament) and the prophets. I have come, not to abolish them, but to fulfill them" (Matthew 5:17). It was the Lamb of God and the Mediator of the new and everlasting covenant speaking. He was the Son of Mary.

Chapter 6

The Great Women of the Bible

Deborah and Jael

Now, let us see how Mary was foreshadowed by some of the great women of the Old Testament. In their prosperity and contentment, the Israelites gradually forgot the goodness of the God who had brought them out of the land of Egypt, and they turned away from him to bow down to the gods of the people who lived around them. These were the false gods called Baal and Asherah. In worshiping them "the children of Israel did evil in the sight of the Lord," and the Lord made them captives of Jabin, king of Canaan. His army was commanded by a great general called Sisera, who had 900 chariots, and for twenty years he cruelly oppressed the children of Israel.

At that time, before there were any kings, Israel was ruled by "judges." It is said that God called them to lead his people whenever they were in danger from their enemies. However, they were more than judges in today's meaning of the term for they were chieftains and heroes as well, and their influence was felt mainly in war. One of the judges of Israel was a woman called Deborah (about 1125 BC). Men at that time did not believe that women should lead the people and the only woman in the Bible who was placed at the height of political power by the common consent of the people was

Deborah. Indeed, there are few women in the history of Israel who have ever attained the public dignity and supreme authority of Deborah. She may be likened to Joan of Arc of later times, who rode in front of the French soldiers and led them to victory.

Deborah's story is told in the first part of the Book of Judges, when the Israelites were about to be attacked by the Canaanites. They were fearful of Sisera and his army of 900 chariots of iron while they had none. When they paled with fear, Deborah sent for a man called Barak from his home in Kedes. He was one of Israel's most capable military men. She let him know that she was not afraid of Sisera and his army, neither was she afraid of his 900 chariots.

She said to him: "Go to Mount Tabor with 10,000 men and I would deliver Sisera with all his soldiers and chariots into your hands." Barak gave a conditional acceptance: "I would go if you accompany me, but not otherwise." Spoken by a man to a woman, this is one of the most unusual passages in the Bible. Deborah agreed to go with him, but she prophesied and warned him that he would gain no honour from the expedition for the Lord will sell Sisera into the hands of a woman. It demonstrates a general with confidence in a woman who had risen to a high place in Israel, largely because of one quality, her abiding faith in God.

At the utterance of Deborah, the tribes under Barak's command rose up against their Canaanite oppressors led by Sisera. The armies met on the slopes of Mount Tabor and Sisera and his chariots were defeated. Sisera himself, however, succeeded in escaping the slaughter. He fled on foot from the battlefield to Kenite territory (the Kenite tribe was a nomadic community, but were well absorbed by Judah). When he reached the tent of Heber the Kenite, he went to Jael, Heber's wife, seeking a hiding place. Jael gave him a warm welcome, but after he had fallen asleep in her tent, battle-weary and drowsy, she stealthily crept up to him, took a tent-peg, grabbed a mallet, and drove a hole right through his temple. On that day Israel was protected by the hand of a woman exactly as prophesied by Deborah.

To celebrate this great victory, the ode of Deborah, one of the earliest martial songs in biblical history, was composed: "That warriors in Israel unbound their hair, that the people came forward with a will, for this bless Yahweh.... Dead, dead were Israel's villages until you rose up, O Deborah; you rose up a mother in Israel.... Blessed be Jael among women; among all women that dwell in tents may she be blessed.... She struck Sisera, crushed his head, pierced his temple and shattered it." (Judges 5:1-31). In the song, Deborah is called "a mother in Israel." She brought peace to the land for forty years. And so, we see in Jael a herald of the woman of Genesis 3;15, who will crush the head of her enemy, Satan. I am referring to Mary, the Woman of Israel, the Mother of all Nations and Queen of Peace, who will usher in the reign of her Son, the King of all Nations and the Prince of Peace.

Judith

The Book of Judith is the history of another victory won by the chosen people over its enemies, thanks to the intervention of another woman. Over a thousand years later, around 125 BC, Jael's story will be told afresh. Judith (her name means "the Jewess") would supplant Jael, but the message would be the same. Two sides are in conflict, that of the people of God and that of the pagan *nations*. God's side seems doomed to extermination, but he intervenes anew to save his people through the hands of a woman.

An Assyrian general, Holofernes, the evil henchman of King Nebuchadnezzar of Babylonia, whose ambition was to lay the whole world at the feet of Nebuchadnezzar and to destroy all other religions, marched against Palestine and laid siege to the city of Bethulia. The city's water supply failed and the people of the city were in such despair that they decided to surrender if no help came within five days. But there lived in that city a young and pious widow named Judith. When she heard that the city would be given up, she called together the leaders and warned them that they were committing a great sin by not trusting in God. She urged them to do penance for this sin. She then went home, put ashes on her head as a sign of penance, and prayed to God for help, asking him to make her strong and brave so that she might save her people.

She then dressed herself in her finest clothes and with one of her maids she went to the enemy camp of the Assyrians and asked to be led to the general. When Holofernes saw her, he was so attracted by her beauty that he commanded that she be allowed to go and come as she wished. Each night Judith prayed that God would guide her in this dangerous work. On the fourth night the general had a dinner for his friends. Lusting for her, he also invited Judith. However, after the feast, the general, overcome with wine, fell into a deep sleep. Judith waited till everybody had left. She stood weeping and praying: "Strengthen me, O Lord, that I may act according to your will." Then taking out the sword of Holofernes, she cut off his head, and gave it to her maid to carry in a bag. They hurriedly left the camp and returned to Bethulia.

In the morning the people of Bethulia hung the head of Holofernes upon the city walls, took up arms and went against the Assyrian camp. When the Assyrians saw the headless body of their general, they were filled with terror and fled. The army of Israel then took courage and attacked and defeated their leaderless enemies. Judith had saved her people.

When Judith brought the head of Holofernes to Bethulia, the song of thanksgiving took up the theme of Deborah's canticle: "May you be blessed, my daughter, by God Most High, beyond all women on earth; and may God be blessed, the Creator of heaven and earth, by whose guidance you cut off the head of the leader of our enemies...." (Judith 13:18). Joachim, the High Priest, and the elders of the Israelites also praised her: " You are the glory of Jerusalem! You are the great pride of Israel! You are the highest honour of our race. By doing all this with your own hand you have deserved well of Israel, and God has approved what you have done. May you be blessed by the Lord Almighty in all the days to come!" (Judith 15:9-11).

The evil Holofernes was decapitated by Judith, and so, once more the Old Testament gives us a prototype of Mary, the woman of Genesis 3:15, the greatest of all the women in the Bible, who was destined to crush the head of the most evil one of all, the ancient serpent. It is the woman "and her seed," who will crush the head of the serpent, as promised by God in the Garden of Eden. But wasn't "her seed," the Redeemer, not foreshadowed several centuries earlier by David when he decapitated the head of the great giant Goliath with the Philistine's own sword? (1 Samuel 17:49-51). "Son of David," cried the blind man, "have pity on me" (John 18:38-39).

Esther

Finally, let us turn to Esther, the great Jewish Queen of Persia. The Hebrew name of the Queen of Persia was Haddassah, meaning "myrtle." Her Persian name, Esther, means "star." Indeed, the ancient writers' opinion of Esther's importance to the story in the Book of Esther becomes apparent, for in this short book of the Old Testament her name appears no less than fifty-five times. Only Sarah, whose name appears as Sarah thirty-five times and as Sarai sixteen times, comes close to this record.

The Book of Esther, like that of Judith, also tells of the deliverance of the nation by the intervention of a woman. The Jews were living in exile in Persia after Jerusalem was sacked by the Babylonians, but they had many enemies. At that time the singular beauty of Esther, a Jewess, attracted the Persian king, Ahasuerus (485-464 BC), and she was taken into his palace, succeeding Vashti as queen. The king, however, did not know that she was Jewish. The Book relates that Haman, a high official in the king's administration, akin to prime minister, resolved to wipe out all the members of the Jewish race throughout the empire of Persia. The date chosen by lot (pur) for this extermination was the 13th day of the 12th month, which is the Hebrew month of Adar. In fact, Haman has been described by modern Jewish writers as a typical Hitler, manifesting an intense hatred for the Jews.

Haman convinced the king of this necessity and the decree for the extermination was signed in the name of King Ahasuerus, sealed with his ring, and letters were sent by runners to every province of the realm, ordering the destruction, slaughter and annihilation of all Jews, young and old, women and children. It was to be on the one day, the 13th day of the 12th month. When Queen Esther's maids told her about it, she was totally overcome with grief. She then sent a message to her uncle Mordecai, a fellow Jew and Benjamite, who was also hated by Haman, and said to him: "Go and assemble all the Jews now in Susa and fast for me. Do not eat or drink, day or night, for three days. For my part, I and my maids would keep the same fast, after which I shall go to the king in spite of the law; and if I perish, I perish." In those days no one could approach the king's chambers without his invitation, not even the queen.

On the third day, when she had finished praying, she took off her mourning attire and dressed herself in her full splendour. Radiant as she was, she then appeared in the presence of the king, whose anger eventually turned into a milder spirit. Although Esther risked her life by appearing before him unannounced, he was so impressed by her beauty and her courage that he rescinded the order and Haman was hanged. Moreover, the Jews were allowed to avenge themselves on the guilty Persians. The king's command and decree came into force on the 13th day of the 12th month, Adar, and so, the day on which the enemies of the Jews had hoped to crush them produced the very opposite effect. It was the Jews who crushed their enemies through the intervention of a woman. To this day an annual feast of rejoicing is held on the 14th and 15th days of Adar. It is the Jewish feast of the Purim, which celebrates the deliverance of the Jews from the pogrom planned by Haman (Esther 3:7, 9:15-32).

Chapter 7

Hail Mary

In the fullness of time the "woman," the greatest of women in the Bible, was born to Joachim and Anne of the tribe of David, a descendant of Abraham. Canon Sheehan was once the parish priest of Doneraile in County Cork, Ireland. Preaching on the Blessed Virgin, he said that it was decreed by God at the fall of our first parents that as their children would have inherited grace and glory if his commands had been obeyed, so, because of their disobedience, their children were to inherit only sin and shame. This law is universal. Not even the greatest saints were exempt from it. Once and once only did God create a soul as pure and beautiful at the moment of its conception as it is now in heaven; a soul to which the Almighty could turn when weary of the deformity which sin had stamped upon mankind. It was the time when the fullness of years had come and it was decreed that the Son should leave the bosom of the Father and take flesh among men.

For centuries, he said, God had not created a soul in grace. Yes, he had fashioned and formed them and sent them into the world, but they were in the power of the enemy before they left his Almighty hands. But now, for an instant, the old time was to come back again when God could look upon his work and say that it was good, and that it did not repent him that he had made it. As St. Bonaventure wrote: "Mary is that being which God cannot make greater. He can make a greater earth and a greater heaven but not a greater mother." Or as Fr. Cyril Papali, O.D. once said: "God exhausted his omnipotence in creating her."

And so, the Blessed Trinity fashioned and formed and sent into the world the soul of Mary. And God admired his handiwork, while hell trembled at the conception of a woman who was destined to break the power of its prince. This is the girl chosen from all women to give God the colour of his eyes and of his hair. She was to teach the Word to speak in her own accent. She was to help the Almighty walk his first baby steps. She was to give him the body and blood in which he would live and suffer and die to redeem us all.

She was called Mary, a famous name in Jewish history, Miriam. Miriam was the sister of Moses, and in God's inscrutable, providential plan, Miriam helped Moses, the leader of the "exodus" from Egyptian slavery, grow. In the New Testament, the new Miriam, Mary, is going to help the Redeemer of the world to grow, to help to save us all. This time it was an "exodus" from the slavery of sin and Satan. Now, as the Gospel of Luke states: "In the sixth month, the angel Gabriel was sent from God to a town of Galilee called Nazareth, to a virgin betrothed to a man named Joseph, of the house of David, and the virgin's name was Mary. And coming to her he said:

> "'Hail, full of grace! The Lord is with you.' But she was greatly troubled by what was said and pondered what sort of greeting this might be. And the angel said to her, 'Do not be afraid, Mary, for you have found favour with God. Behold, you will conceive in your womb, and bear a son, and you shall name him Jesus. He will be great and will be called Son of the Most High, and the Lord God will give him the throne of David his father, and he will rule over the house of Jacob forever, and of his kingdom there will be no end'" (Luke 1:26-34).

Let us now research in detail the deep significance and meaning attached to the angel's greeting, a salutation which was so precious to Mary while she was here, and now in eternity.

"Hail"

Literally, the Greek word *Chaire* means "Joy to you" or "Rejoice." The Latin Vulgate translation is *Ave*, meaning "Hail," but reading *Chaire* as "Rejoice" instead of as "Hail" has been disputed. The Jerusalem Bible accepts "Rejoice," whereas the New American Bible prefers "Hail."

"Full of Grace"

Now, the same Gabriel who greeted Mary with the word *Chaire* completes the salutation calling her *kecharitomene (*full of grace). *Gratia plena* is how it is rendered by the Vulgate. "Full of grace," he said to her. It is noteworthy that none of the great women of the Old Testament has been called "full of grace." "This solemn and unparalleled salutation," said Pope Pius IX, "heard at no other time, shows the *Mother of God* as the seat of all divine graces, and as adorned with all the gifts of the divine Spirit (*Ineffabilis Deus*).

Indeed, most Catholic theologians agree with the Dominican Suarez in holding that "if we add up all the graces conferred on all the saints and angels in one, it would not equal Mary's grace." Such is the excess of their interpretation of the meaning of "full of grace." May I add that my choice of the word "excess" is in no way intended to mean "undue excess." The great theologian and Doctor of the Church, St. Thomas Aquinas, was equally exuberant: "There is no doubt that the Blessed Virgin received in a supereminent degree the gifts of wisdom, of miracles, and even of prophecy." Augustine also justified the privilege: "We know that she has received such an abundance of grace because she was worthy to conceive and bring forth God." And so, "full of grace" she was.

"The Lord is with you"

The *Dominus Tecum (*The Lord is with you) is an expression that is prominent in the vocabulary of the Old Testament. However, outside of the case of the Annunciation, the *Dominus tecum* was never addressed to a woman. The only exception was Judith. It signifies the assistance given by God to the individual whom he deputes to accomplish a great work. And so, when Yahweh is with his people, victory is certain. As the psalm says: "With Yahweh on my side, I fear nothing: what can man do to me?" (Psalm 118:6). This remark of God was first said in the promise to Isaac: "Fear not, for *I am with you* and will bless you and multiply your descendants for my servant Abraham's sake" (Genesis 26:24). And to Jacob Yahweh also said: "*I am with you* and will keep you wherever you go ... for I will not leave you until I have done that of which I have spoken to you" (Genesis 28:15).

When Moses at the burning bush fears going to the Pharaoh, Yahweh also fortifies him: "I am who I am ... *I will be with you*" (Exodus 3:11-12). As successor to Moses and the one chosen to lead Israel into the Promised Land, Joshua is also assured: "You shall bring the children of Israel into the land ... *I will be with you*" (Deuteronomy 31:23). In similar vein, Gideon, son of Joash, was called to liberate his people from the Midianites. Yahweh promised: "*I shall be with you* and you will crush Midian as though it were a single man" (Judges 6:11-17). Jeremiah, too, was called by the Lord to be a prophet to the nations but wished to decline the invitation because he was fearful. But he is consoled by the Lord: "*I am with you* to protect you" (Jeremiah 1:6-8).

And so, "*the Lord is with you*" speaks of the protection of God for his chosen ones and not just the actual presence of God. It was the divine assurance to those who have been called but who had to put up with difficulties in accepting the mission entrusted to them. But for God to be with his people, his people had to be with him. As Moses said to the Israelites in his last discourse before he died: "You are a people sacred to the Lord, your God; he has chosen you from all the *nations* on the face of the earth to be a people peculiarly his own. It was not because you were the largest of all *nations* that the Lord set his heart on you and chose you, for you are really the smallest of all *nations*. It was because the Lord loved you and because of his fidelity to the oath he has sworn to your fathers, that he brought you out with his strong hand from the place of slavery, and ransomed you from the hand of Pharaoh, king of Egypt. Understand, then, that the Lord, your God, is God indeed, the faithful God who keeps his merciful covenant down to the thousandth generation, towards those who love him and keep his commandments, but who repays with destruction the person who hates him...." (Deuteronomy 7:6-10).

"Blessed Are You Among Women"

After Gabriel told her that her cousin Elizabeth had also conceived a son in her old age, "Mary set out at that time and went as quickly as she could to a town in the hill country of Judah. She went into Zechariah's house and greeted Elizabeth. Elizabeth was filled with the Holy Spirit and said loudly:

> *"Of all women you are the most blessed, and blessed is the fruit of your womb"* (Luke 1:39-42).

The expression "blessed are you among women" occurred for the first time in the canticle of Deborah (Judges 5:2-31). It was addressed to Jael, the wife of Heber, the Kenite (see chapter 6). Jael it was who took a tent-peg and with a mallet drove a hole right through the temple of Israel's dreaded enemy, Sisera. It is this feat that Deborah, one of the judges of Israel, celebrated, saying: "Blessed among women be Jael, blessed among tent-dwelling women" (Judges 5:24). Over a thousand years later, Jael's story will be told afresh in Judith who brings the gory head of Holofernes to Bethulia, whereupon Ozias, the prince of the people of Israel, said to her: "Blessed are you, O daughter, by the Lord, the Most High God, above all women upon the earth" (Judith 13:22-23).

In the New Testament, Luke 1:42 records the words of Gabriel to Mary: "Of all women you are the *most* blessed...." (Jerusalem Bible). In saying that Mary is not merely blessed but the *most* blessed among all women, Luke thereby seems to be pointing out that it is she in whom God will bring the salvation of his people to fulfillment. Mary not only supplants Jael and Judith, she also stands on a higher plain. Mary is the woman *most* blessed among all women because only she was chosen in a unique way to become the *Mother of God,* through whom salvation would be wrought. This praise is to be perpetuated down the centuries as Mary prophesied: "From henceforth all generations will call me blessed" (Luke 1:48).

"Blessed is the fruit of your Womb"

The women of the Old Testament are usually associated with fruitfulness — but not always. Indeed, an "unfruitful womb and dry breasts" (Hosea 9:14) will appear to be a sign of divine rejection, and it is ironical, though not by chance, that the father of a multitude of descendants, Abraham himself, and after him, his son Isaac and his grandson Jacob, had wives who were barren. Consider also, Hannah with Samuel, and the parents of Samson. And so, the history of this people who were to become as numberless as the sands on the seashore and the stars of heaven (Genesis 16:2; 25:21; 29:31) was destined to begin with the very barrenness of Sarah, Rebecca, and Rachel!

Was it a sign that we must trust in him that God chose the sorrow and humiliation of the childless woman as a setting in which the promise would be fulfilled? As Lucien Deiss said in his book *Mary, Daughter of Sion,* it is the very barrenness and sorrow of Sarah that God was trying to form into a wellspring of fruitfulness and joy for Abraham. The barren wife becomes the joyful *mother of nations* (Isaiah 54:1-3).

We can see now how the miraculous fruitfulness of Abraham and Sarah serves as a preparation for the miraculous fruitfulness of Mary. Sarah was unable to have children because she was barren and had passed the age of childbearing. Mary could not have a child because she "knew not man" and, according to tradition and the mystics, she had resolved to remain a virgin ever since her sojourn in the temple at an early age. Yet it is through Mary that Abraham and Sarah became the foreparents of Jesus. And so, the long series of generations, coming down through the entire history of the chosen people, was then brought to final issue in the Son of God (Matthew 1:1-2, 15-16).

In Mary, therefore, the ancient prophecy of Moses to the Israelites in the Book of Deuteronomy is fulfilled: "As your reward for heeding these decrees and observing them carefully, the Lord, your God, will keep with you the merciful covenant which he promised on oath to your fathers. He will love and bless and multiply you; he will bless the *fruit of your womb....*" (Deuteronomy 7:13).

Chapter 8

The Virgin Says Yes

Now, when she said "yes" to the invitation of God's ambassador to be the Mother of the Word, she immediately became the bride of the Holy Spirit. He overshadowed her and at that moment she conceived the God-man, the Redeemer. Redemption had begun. It was the marriage between heaven and earth. And so, with her, in her, and through her the Holy Spirit produced his most illustrious work, the Incarnation of the Word. The hypostatic union of the Son of God with human nature was accomplished and fulfilled.

Indeed, with her consent she played her part in what may be called "God's conspiracy" to save the world from the dominion of Satan. It was the beginning of the "Good News," but it was bad news for Satan. The woman of Genesis 3:15 had consented, and with her consent two wondrous things happened. A woman while remaining virgin became a mother, and more wondrous yet, a woman became the mother of her own Creator. As St. Francis of Assisi once said: "O humble sublimity! O sublime humility!"

The first Eve said "yes" to Satan and sin. The second Eve said "yes" to Gabriel and God. The first Eve was disobedient. The second Eve was obedient. It was a fruit which hung from a tree in the Garden of Eden which Satan used to bring death to mankind. It would be the fruit of her womb which hung from a tree on Calvary which God would use to restore life to humanity. The situation would be reversed. Death through the first Eve; life through the second Eve. Man's friendship with God would be restored.

Genesis 1:26 says: "Let us make man to our image and likeness …" It was the Trinity speaking, Father, Son and Holy Spirit. But in the family of man there is a father, a mother, and their offspring. And so, God, who in eternity dwelled in the bosom of the Father without a Mother, would in time dwell in the bosom of a mother without a father. God then created his own mother through the Second Person of the Holy Trinity, who took upon himself flesh and became man — while still remaining God. The problem was solved.

Now, he could have entered the world as a grown man as did the first Adam, but he chose otherwise. Infinity chose to confine himself in the womb of a mere mortal woman and the angels must have gasped in wonderment. The bodiless takes upon himself a body; the invisible makes himself visible; he who is without beginning begins; the Son of God becomes Son of Man. And prophecy is fulfilled.

She was the sole human parent. No human father was involved and she alone furnished the sacred body of her Son. This body would be the instrument of redemption, for redemption was to come from suffering. And just as the Son came eternally from the substance of the Father alone, so, too, in time, he came from the flesh and blood of Mary alone. As Fr. Michael O'Carrol of Dublin so scientifically put it: "His very genetic substance and constitution was Marian. His DNA was totally Marian. He was the first Marian." They both had the bloodline of Abraham and David.

She then became the Womb of God, the House of God, the Tabernacle of the Most High, the Ark of the Covenant, or more correctly, the living Ark of the Mediator of the New Covenant. Moses was the mediator of the Old Covenant with the people of Israel. And just as the ancient ark of Mosaic times was covered inside and outside with the purest gold, so is she pure, precious, and regal for she is the Queen of heaven and earth. The ancient ark was made of an incorruptible acacia wood, so was she incorrupt and incorruptible, and, as the Church teaches, did not experience the corruption of the grave. The ancient ark contained the two tablets of the Law given to Moses on Mt. Sinai, but she contained in her womb not the tablets of the Law but the Law-giver himself. The ark contained a ciborium with some of the miraculous manna which fell from heaven to feed the Israelites on their journey to the Promised Land. However, with her "yes," she then contained within her womb, not the bread which the Israelites ate and yet they died, but the true Bread of Life which brings everlasting life to mankind.

John quotes the words of Jesus himself: *"I tell you most solemnly, it was not Moses who gave you bread from heaven, the true bread; for the bread of God is that which comes down from heaven and gives life to the world* (John 6:32-34). *"I am the bread of life.... Your fathers ate manna in the desert and they are dead; but this is the bread which has come down from heaven. Anyone who eats this bread will live forever...."* (John 6:48-51). Nine months later, she gave birth to the God-man, the second Adam, bone of her bones and flesh of her flesh, as Adam said about Eve. There was no room in the inn and so he was born in a stable, for where else should a lamb be born, even the Lamb of God, he, who was the most humble of all the lambs? He was born in Bethlehem and so should it also be. Bethlehem means "House of bread." And from her breasts she gave milk to this Bread of Life.

But let us now turn to the gratitude which she expressed to God for extending that invitation to her to be the mother of his Son.

Chapter 9

The Magnificat

The Old Testament Hannah, the wife of Elcana, was barren because "the Lord had closed her womb" (1 Samuel 1:6), and she prayed to Yahweh: "O Lord of hosts, if only you will look down on the affliction of your servant and will be mindful of me, and not forget your handmaid, and will give to your servant a male child ..." (1 Samuel 1:11). Yahweh was indeed mindful of Hannah. She gave birth to Samuel, the last of the judges and the first of the prophets. When she came to the temple to offer and consecrate him, her first-born, to Yahweh, her prayer of thanksgiving was:

> *"My heart has rejoiced in the Lord ... because I have joy in your salvation. There is none holy as the Lord is ... and there is none strong like our God ... the bow of the mighty is overcome, and the weak are girth with strength. They that were full before have hired out themselves for bread: and the hungry are filled.... The Lord makes poor and makes rich, he humbles and he exalts...."* (1 Samuel 2:1-10).

When at the "Visitation," Elizabeth said to Mary that she was "blessed" for trusting that the Lord's words to her would be fulfilled (Luke 1:45), Mary proclaimed and praised the greatness of the Lord in what may be considered the first Christian hymn. It is called the *Magnificat* (Latin for '*magnifies*'), and is the song of thanksgiving *par excellence* in the New Testament. As Pope John Paul II once said: "It is the Song of Songs of the New Testament." It is an echo of Hannah's prayer of thanksgiving in the Old Testament.

> *"Then Mary said: 'My soul magnifies the Lord, and my spirit rejoices in God my saviour; because he has regarded the lowliness of his handmaid; for behold, from henceforth all generations shall call me blessed; because he who is mighty has done great things for me, and holy is his name; and his mercy is from generation to generation on those who fear him. He has shown might with his arm, he has scattered the proud in the conceit of their heart. He has put down the mighty from their thrones, and has exalted the lowly. He has filled the hungry with good things, and the rich he has sent away empty. He has given help to Israel, his servant, mindful of his mercy — even as he spoke to our fathers — to Abraham and to his posterity'"* (Luke 1:46-55).

There are other passages in the Old Testament in which we encounter this first verse of the *Magnificat*. One of them is in the canticle of Habakkuk: "But I will rejoice in Yahweh, I will exult in God my saviour" (Habakkuk 3:18). Another verse in the Old Testament which heralds the "joy" of the first verse of the *Magnificat* is found in the first poem of Isaiah: "I exult for joy in Yahweh, my soul rejoices in my God, for he has clothed me in the garments of salvation...." (Isaiah 61:10-11).

Mary also calls God "her Saviour" for like every other creature she too needs him. She recognizes that God, who has a preferential love for the poor, has chosen the poorest of the poor, herself, a young virgin, to make her his handmaid; she, who dwells in a little unknown village and has neither pride nor power nor riches. And so, the almighty Lord enters into the world through the porchway of humility and poverty.

> *"From henceforth all generations shall call me blessed."*

She herself can speak in all humility of how all generations will call her "blessed" for she knows that the blessing would only lead to God and never remain fixed in herself. She knows that the messianic age is beginning in her, and her song of thanksgiving is addressed to Jesus the Saviour, whom she is carrying in her womb. It is because of this maternity that generations of *nations* will proclaim her "blessed." In other words, she was fully aware of the greatness of her mission, but at the same time she fully recognized herself to be "a lowly servant."

But a similar prophecy of "blessedness" was addressed to the entire "people of the promise" by the prophet Malachi. His name means "my messenger." Speaking of Israel, the Book of Malachi reads: "Then all the *nations* will call you *blessed* for you will be a delightful land," said the Lord of hosts" (Malachi 3:12). Was this also not a herald of the Woman of Israel and the *Mother of all Nations, Mary*?

> *"Because he who is mighty has done great things for me and holy is his name."*

Mary is also saying here that her *Magnificat* renders all glory to Holy God for the great things which he has accomplished in her — the incarnation of her Son. She does not claim for herself any merit or glory, for that would be contrary to her spirit of poverty and humility. As Leviticus 19:2 states: "Yahweh spoke to Moses; he said: 'Be holy, for I, Yahweh your God, am holy.'" And so, "holy is his name."

> *"And his mercy is from generation to generation on those who fear him.... He has given help to Israel, his servant, mindful of his mercy — even as he spoke to our fathers — to Abraham and to his posterity forever."*

What she is saying here is that the God of mercy has come to the help of Israel, his servant, and through Israel, to the help of all mankind. It began with Abraham and by extension all Israel, and through Mary this same mercy is going to be passed on to all the world in Jesus Christ and his body, the Church. And so she is called the Mother of Mercy. It is also the old saying: "Salvation comes from the Jews" (John 4:22). This verse of the *Magnificat* also borrows words from David's psalm: "Bless the Lord; O my soul and all my being, bless his holy name.... Merciful and gracious is the Lord, slow to anger and abounding in kindness.... But the kindness of the Lord is from eternity to eternity toward those who fear him" (Psalm 103:1-17).

> *"He has shown might with his arm, he has scattered the proud in the conceit of their heart. He has put down the mighty from their thrones, and has exalted the lowly. He has filled the hungry with good things and the rich he has sent away empty."*

It may also be said that the Virgin Mary is here preparing us for the entry of Christ in the temple to overturn the tables of the money-changers, and for his grave indictment against the rich, "who already have their human reward." Indeed, the *Magnificat* can be seen as the herald of the eight Beatitudes and that she is thus providing a platform for the Sermon on the Mount in which her Son will proclaim blessedness to the poor, the meek, the afflicted and the needy, to those who show mercy, to the pure, to the peaceful and to the persecuted. It is a constant theme in the Gospel.

And so, this canticle of Mary is ingeniously replete with biblical references from the Old Testament. It gives witness to one who is living in close contact with the history of her people and with the Scripture with which she is so familiar. She is 'full of grace' and undoubtedly she was given the gifts of extraordinary wisdom and knowledge and therefore must have known the Scriptures page by page, verse by verse. Here we see how well-versed in the Hebrew Bible she was, and how deeply her whole being is rooted in the themes of the Old Testament. She expresses her joy in a selection of passages borrowed from the Scriptures. She tells us the story of the New Testament with the text of the Old.

Mary's magnificent *Magnificat* can therefore be seen as composed of three parts: a song of praise, a song of the poor of Yahweh, and the fulfillment of the promise made to Abraham. In fact, the whole meaning of the *Magnificat* may be summed up in one theme:

God loves the poor, the Messiah wills to be born of a poor and humble Virgin, and his mercy is limitless.

And now, a surprise for modern-day Protestants, many of whom do not seem to know that the great Protestant reformer himself, Martin Luther, had a deep appreciation of Mary's *Magnificat.* In his commentary on the *Magnificat,* Luther wrote: "O blessed Virgin and Mother of God, how have you been able to be considered as nothing, and disdained as of little consequence, and yet God has nonetheless regarded you with all his grace and all his riches, and accomplished in you such mighty things? Yet, you are blessed from this hour and unto all eternity, you who have found such a God ..." (*Mariae Lobgesang,* Wittenberg, March 10, 1521).

Karl Barth (1886-1968), the celebrated Swiss Protestant theologian, also added his praise of Mary: "'Behold from henceforth all generations shall call me blessed.' What unspeakable grandeur there is in this encounter!... If ever in the history of the world anything of great importance has taken place it is in this regard. Here there is no hesitation, no fear, no light, which runs the risk of being extinguished, but rather, certitude. Victory has already been won. Our calling is to be on the side of Mary.... We have only one thing to do, like Mary: to let God act. Let it be unto me as you have said" (Bible Studies in the First Chapter of St. Luke in *Foi et vie,* 85-6, p. 509-10, 1936).

Chapter 10

The Sufferer and the Co-Sufferer

Thirty years after the Virgin said "yes," the mother and her Son were invited to a wedding banquet, but the bride and groom were embarrassed. There was no more wine. The guests were obviously enjoying themselves immensely! It was then that she initiated her role as Mediatrix with the one Mediator, and as Advocate for the people. "They have no wine," she told her Son. But she knew full well that by initiating his public ministry she would be hastening what she always feared most — his Calvary. But, undoubtedly, inspired by the Holy Spirit, she knew that the time had come: *"Woman, what have I to do with thee? My hour is not yet come,"* he said to her. His mother, as it were, disregarded him and turned to the servants, and said: "Do whatever he tells you." It was then that he turned water, not only into wine, but into the best wine — six jars full, about 120 gallons of it (John 2:12). It was as though heavenly protocol demanded that it was his mother who should initiate his public ministry.

Maundy Thursday Night

Three years later, as his ministry was approaching its end, and at another banquet which we call the Last Supper, he performed his last miracle on earth. This time he changed wine into his blood, and bread into his body: *"Take this and eat. This is my body which will be given up for you.... Take this and drink. This is the cup of my blood, the blood of the new and everlasting covenant. It will be shed for you and for all so that sins will be forgiven"* (Matthew 26:26-28).

She is hardly mentioned in the Gospels for it is the Gospel of her Son, the Gospel of Jesus, not of Mary. She is not there, for example, on Tabor, where he manifested himself in all his glory to Peter, James and John (John 9:1-8). She is not there on that Sunday when the crowds waved palms and shouted hosannas (Luke 19:37). This was not her place. Her place was on Calvary, where she stood under the Cross for three hours and watched the bloody immolation of her Son. *Stabat mater dolorosa*, we say in Latin.

The Night of the Passover

But all this was foretold in the Old Testament. It is recorded that when God heard the cry of the Israelites and decided to free them from Egyptian bondage, he decreed that a young lamb without blemish, a one-year-old male, was to be slaughtered and some of its blood daubed on the doorposts of their houses. The Israelites were to eat the lamb hurriedly that same night with unleavened bread and bitter herbs, for the Lord was to pass through the land of Egypt that night and strike down every first born (Exodus 12:1-14).

Now, in Old Testament times almost all things, according to the Law, were cleansed with blood and without the shedding of blood there was no remission. And so, by the sacrifice and the blood of the paschal lamb the Hebrews were delivered from Egyptian slavery (but not from sin). In the New Testament, however, the blood of Christ was to replace the animal covenant blood of Moses' time. As is written in Hebrews 10:4-10, Paul said: "Bulls' blood and goats' blood are useless for taking away sin, and this is what he (Christ) said on coming into the world: *'You who wanted no sacrifice or oblation, prepared a body for me. You took no pleasure in holocausts or sacrifices for sin*; then I said, just as I was commanded in the scroll of the book, 'God, here I am! I am coming to obey your will.'"

The lamb had to be male, for Christ, the true Paschal Lamb of God, was of that sex. It was one year old to foretell that Christ would be sacrificed in the flower of his youth. It had to be without spot or blemish to reflect the sinlessness of Christ. The Israelites fled from Egypt at night and were delivered from slavery to foretell how the Lord would be arrested at night to be sacrificed and to deliver the world from slavery to Satan (Exodus 12:1-49). The lamb's blood sprinkled on the doorposts pointed to Jesus' blood splattered on the Cross, except that the killing of the unblemished lamb on that historic night in Egypt was merciful when compared to the dreadful passion and crucifixion of the true Lamb of God, who voluntarily chose for himself the most painful and agonizing of deaths: *"The Father loves me, because I lay down my life in order to take it up again. No one takes it from me; I lay it down of my own free will"* (John 10:18).

Yahweh also decreed to Moses that the lamb must be eaten in one house but not a bone must be broken (Exodus 12:46-47). And so, while the soldiers would break the legs of the two thieves, not one bone of the true Lamb was broken (John 19:33-34). His skin was all torn off by the flagellation, his blood and serum oozing out and then clotted, made it look as though he had been roasted like the lamb was on the night of the Exodus from Egypt. This was the true portrait of Jesus on the Cross, not the aesthetic and comfortable-looking figure which is depicted on crucifixes today. It was not at all like that. It was a savage slaughter, a cruel carnage, a merciless murder. The Shroud of Turin loudly testifies to this mutilation. It is the *raison d'être* of this miraculous cloth.

About 1300 years after the sacrifice of the paschal lamb in Egypt, Jesus, the true Lamb of God, was crucified, and at the moment the Cross was lifted up on Calvary, the temple resounded with the blast of trumpets which were always blown to announce the sacrifice of the paschal lambs in the temple courtyard. Prophecy was being fulfilled. The sacrifice of Isaac (see chapter 4) was renewed on Calvary. But whereas on the Mount of Moriah God supplied the victim (a ram) to be substituted for Isaac and spared both the life of the son and the hearts of his father Abraham and his mother Sarah, on Calvary God fully accepted both the sacrifice of his Son and the broken heart of his mother, Mary, the second Eve, the Ewe who witnessed her lamb slaughtered as she stood by helplessly.

At three o'clock in the afternoon, the customary hour of the sacrifice and death of the paschal lamb in the Jewish ritual in the temple ever since Solomon's time, the true Lamb of God died. At that moment the temple veil in front of the empty Holy of Holies (the Ark of the Covenant was since lost) was torn from top to bottom and an earthquake toppled the two pillars which held the veil, depicting the end of the old dispensation and the ushering of the new Covenant (Matthew 27:51-54). Scholars of biblical history have calculated that it was the "first Friday" in the month of April in 33 AD. The old Covenant was ratified with the blood of animals. The new Covenant was ratified with the blood of Jesus.

But about 740 years before the birth of Jesus, Isaiah did accurately prophesy the passion and death of the Lamb of God: "He was pierced through for our faults, crushed for our sins. On him lies a punishment that brings us peace, and through his wounds we are healed. We had all gone astray like sheep; each taking his own way, and Yahweh burdened him with the sins of all of us. Harshly dealt with, he bore it humbly, he never opened his mouth, like a lamb that is led to the slaughter house, like a sheep that is dumb before its shearer, never opening its mouth" (Isaiah 53:5-7).

But even before the time of Isaiah, David's Psalm 22 also prophesied the type of death of the Messiah: "My God, my God, why have you deserted me? ... I am like water draining away, my bones are all disjointed, my heart is like wax, melting inside me, my palate is drier than a potsherd and my tongue is stuck to my jaw.... I can count every one of my bones, and there they glare at me, gloating; they divide my garments among them and cast lots for my clothes." Indeed, after reading the Scriptures I find it most inexplicable that Judaism refuses to recognize Jesus as the Messiah!

The Co-Sufferer

In 1373, Lady Julian of Norwich, in her book *Revelations of Divine Love,* which records her privileged visions from God, says of Mary: "I saw part of the love and suffering of Our Lady Saint

Mary, for she and Christ were so joined in love that the greatness of their love caused the greatness of her grief ... for the higher, the greater, and the sweeter the love is, so the greater the grief is for those who love, to see their loved one suffer." But how can words describe and measure Mary's anguish on that day? Perhaps it can be appreciated somewhat better if every mother were to contemplate her own son on the cross in place of the Son of Mary. Yet if there were a thousand such mothers standing at the feet of a thousand crosses bearing their thousand crucified sons, the sum total of their anguish could not in any way measure the pain and suffering of that *Mother of Sorrows* on that hill on that Friday that some men call "Good."

However, what, unfortunately, is also not appreciated by many is that spiritual and mental suffering can be as agonizing as physical pain, and at times even more so. For example, the emotional pain of the depressive patient, the spiritual dryness of the "desert" and the dark night of the soul, which some people experience, can parallel or exceed physical pain, albeit measured on different scales and parameters of human suffering. There are also many cases, for example, of elderly spouses of happy and long-standing marriages, dying within hours or days of each other from the sheer anguish of the death of a loved one and from the unbearable and emotional pain of the separation. So it would have been with the Mother of Love on that Friday had she not been preserved from death by God.

Redemption came from suffering, and so, it was the Redeemer on the Cross and the Co-Redemptrix (who gave him his body, the very instrument of redemption), standing beneath the Cross throughout the long ordeal. Three hours later, and close to his death, he made his last will and testament and bequeathed his mother to be our mother also, our spiritual mother, just as Yahweh is our spiritual Father and Jesus is our spiritual brother. *"Woman, behold your son.... Behold your mother,"* he said to his mother and then to John (John 19:26-27). It was then that she officially became the *Mother of Mankind*, the *Mother of all Nations*.

"Woman, behold your son," he said to her. He was obviously referring to her as the "woman" first spoken of in Genesis 3:15: "I will put enmity between you and the woman, and between your seed and her seed; she will crush your head." It was on this hill

called Calvary that this verse in Genesis was fulfilled. The word Calvary is from the Latin word *Calvaria*, meaning skull. The Cross of the Redeemer was firmly dug into it. The hill was also called Golgotha, the Hebrew word from the Greek *Kranion,* a skull. And so, the "skull" was "crushed" by the man on the Cross, the Redeemer ("her seed"), and beneath that rugged Cross was the Co-Redemptrix; one suffering woman, suffering *with* God who in turn was suffering *for* mankind and *from* them.

In October 1920, in a private apparition to the saintly Berthe Petit, a visionary, highly respected in ecclesiastic and lay societies in Belgium, Jesus is said to have exalted the merits of the sorrow of his mother, saying: "The title 'Immaculate' belongs to the whole being of my mother and not specifically to her heart. This title flows from my gratuitous gift to the Virgin who has given me birth. However, my mother has acquired for her heart the title 'Sorrowful' by sharing generously in all the sufferings of my heart and my body from the crib to the Cross. There is not one of these sorrows which did not pierce the heart of my mother. Living image of my crucified body, her virginal flesh bore the invisible marks of my wounds as her heart felt the sorrows of my own. Nothing could ever tarnish the incorruptibility of her immaculate heart. The title of 'Sorrowful' belongs, therefore, to the heart of my mother, and, more than any other, this title is dear to her because it springs from the union of her heart with mine in the redemption of humanity. This title has been acquired by her through her full participation in my Calvary, and it should precede the gratuitous title 'Immaculate' which my love bestowed upon her by a singular *privilege."*

But it was as though God had predetermined that one had to be a "Mary" to have the *privilege* of standing beneath the Cross. John speaks of that congregation: "Standing by the cross were his mother (Mary), and his mother's sister, Mary the wife of Clopas, and Mary Magdalene" (John 19:25).

Of course, this human sacrifice of the Son of the Most High was not God's reward to mankind for our faithfulness and virtue, for man's history was one of sin, disloyalty and ingratitude. What inspired the Incarnation and the sacrifice on Calvary was not man's merit, therefore, but God's love and infinite mercy. St. Thomas Aquinas in his *Summa Theologica* explained why God became man.

He said that when man rebelled against God, God's justice required that adequate reparation be made, but since God is infinite, an infinite insult was made to him. However, justice also required that the reparation be offered by man, but man is a finite being and incapable of making infinite reparation. The only solution to the impasse was that the infinite God should become man, and as man offer reparation to God. So in his loving mercy, God sent his Son to make reparation for the sin of man: "God so loved the world that he gave his only begotten Son...." (John 3:16).

Chapter 11

The Shroud of Turin – True or False?

Crucifixion was an utterly painful and degrading punishment which subjected the victim to the utmost indignity. Indeed, it has been described as a form of execution which vividly manifests the demonic character of human cruelty. This was aggravated further by the fact that quite often the victims were never buried but served as food for wild beasts and birds of prey. In this way the humiliation was complete. In Roman times it was usually executed on dangerous criminals and members of the lowest classes. And so, in the death of Jesus Christ, God identified himself with the utter extreme of human wretchedness. He died like a common criminal in torment on a tree of shame.

Ian Wilson, in his book *The Blood and the Shroud,* states that many authors, sceptical of the Shroud's authenticity, write of it as the "shroud" rather than the "Shroud," arguing that any author who uses an upper-case "Shroud" must automatically be a true believer. If this is so, he stated that he himself was very happy to use upper-case "S." Yet there are some true believers who use an upper-case "S," but use a lower-case "c" for the Cross of Christ. I find it difficult to accept that the Cross is not as important as the Shroud. And so, I also use a capital "C" for the Cross.

Now, the Shroud of Turin bears an image corresponding impressively with the Gospel account of the Passion of Christ. It made its first appearance in 1355 at Lirey in northern France. In 1453, it was acquired by Louis I, the Duke of Savoy, and his descendants at first preserved it in Chambery, the capital of his domains, and later, in 1502, it was kept in Sainte-Chapelle Church. One year after the Blessed Virgin appeared in Guadalupe, Mexico, in 1531, and left her miraculous image on the tilma of Juan Diego, during the night of December 3-4, 1532, fire broke out in the choir-sacristy of Sainte-Chapelle, which almost destroyed the Shroud. One side of the silver box containing the folded cloth became so hot due to the high temperature, that a drop of metal, melting from the lid, poured through small areas of the cloth.

On September 14, 1578, Duke Emmanuel Philbert transferred the Shroud to Turin, and it was placed in a shrine in the presbytery of Turin Cathedral until the chapel of the Shroud was built in the Cathedral of St. John the Baptist. It was permanently installed in the chapel there on June 1, 1694. In 1983, King Umberto II, the last king of Italy, bequeathed the Shroud to the Pope before he died. In fact, it is often not realized that the Shroud has only been owned by the Roman Catholic Church for the last fifteen years through the person of Pope John Paul II.

This Shroud is unique. There is no other burial linen in existence that bears the image of a crucified man. In fact, no other burial cloth with similar markings has turned up anywhere. It is of pure flax, as has been confirmed by analysis of the threads under the optic microscope and the scanning electron microscope. There is no trace of any organic or inorganic coloring pigments on the cloth, nor of any chemical compound extraneous to the flax fibers. The imprints on the Shroud are therefore the result of a natural process which has still to be explained. Inexplicably also, only the surface fibers are involved in the forming of the image, which is seen only on one side of the cloth. Indeed, even in this 20th century, despite all scientific advances, we still do not know how to produce a result of this kind.

Another very unique property of the Shroud image is that it is indelible. This is shown by the fact that despite the vagaries and documented vicissitudes in the Shroud's history, the imprint is as vivid today as it was over the centuries, whereas artificial images are unstable and in time disappear. It has been the same for the image of the Blessed Virgin on the tilma of Juan Diego in Guadalupe.

The imprints on the Shroud of Turin are those of a human corpse in a pronounced state of *rigor mortis*. He is just under six feet tall and of good physique. Images of the front and back of the head nearly touch in the middle of the cloth, suggesting that the man was laid on his back on the bottom half of the linen and the other half was drawn over his face and front. The fact that there is absolutely no evidence of decomposition of the body suggests that he was in the Shroud for less than forty-eight hours, in keeping with the Gospel account. Of course, to Christian believers, the absence of decomposition of the body presents no mystery what-soever, for although Christ's death was part of the divine plan, decomposition was not.

The image bears the marks of lacerations from a severe scourg-ing and a badly bruised and swollen, but nonetheless dignified, face. The chest cavity is expanded as of someone agonizing for hours to inhale air into his lungs. As for the crown of thorns, it was not a wreath-like circlet as is commonly depicted. Instead it was a crude cap covering the entire skull, and its thorns dug into the scalp vessels which are well-known to bleed profusely. There are thirteen blood flows which can be traced to puncture wounds on the head.

The knees of the man on the Shroud also revealed extensive damage such as would be incurred through heavy falls. There were also two oval areas of excoriations in the region of the left and right shoulders, caused by the carrying of the patibulum or the cross-beam of the Cross. There was also clear evidence that nails were driven into the wrists and not the palms of the hand. Appar-ently, when the nail had pierced a certain anatomical space in the wrist it damaged the median nerve, which caused the thumb to flex inward against the palms. And so, no thumbs are visible on the Shroud image!

A nail was also driven between the second and third metatarsal bones with the left foot on top of the right. In addition to puncture wounds in the wrists and feet, there was a gaping hole between the fifth and sixth ribs on the right side, and upon close examination, clear serous fluid is seen mixed with the blood which flowed from the incision. Amazingly, with all of this violent puncturing, as the Scripture predicted, not a bone was broken!

The Roman Flagrum

The Shroud also testifies that all across the back, shoulders, buttocks and legs there were severe welts and shredding of the skin from flagellations with the Roman *flagrum*. This was a short-handled whip with two or three loose cords, hooked and tipped with metal dumbbells or pieces of bone, and which dug into the flesh at every stroke. It is documented that whenever a thorough whipping was carried out, the *flagrum* rained blood across the courtyard. The direction of the scourges on the Shroud also testifies that two soldiers stood, feet apart, on either side of Jesus, swishing their whips. How long this took, no one really knows, but experts have counted up to 120 lashes on the Shroud's image.

The German mystic, stigmatist and visionary Anne Catherine Emmerich (1774-1824) bore the wounds of Christ towards the end of her life. She ate no food save Holy Communion and was in ecstasy on many occasions. It was during these ecstasies that she witnessed in visions the details of Our Lord's life, which were recorded in her diary, *The Dolorous Passion of Our Lord Jesus Christ*. According to her, the scourging lasted for over half an hour. In her chapter on the flagellation, she wrote: "Two ruffians continued to strike Our Lord with unremitting violence for quarter of an hour, and were then succeeded by two others. His body was entirely covered with black, blue, and red marks; the blood trickling down to the ground. These two recommenced the scourging with even greater fury. He looked at his torturers with his eyes filled with blood as if entreating mercy, but their brutality appeared to have increased."

Molds and Pollens

Professor Pierluigi Baima-Bollone, an Italian forensic expert, after analyzing full threads that he had extracted from the Shroud's tiny blood stains, claims to have positively identified human blood of the group AB. Indeed, this was the most common blood group of the Jews in Israel at that time. The Shroud was also found to contain different kinds of pollen and large quantities of molds. We know that the Shroud appeared in Europe in the late Middle Ages and a remarkable number of pollen grains identified on the Shroud has been found to belong to species found in Palestine, the Arab lands of Asia Minor, and in Savoy and Piedmont, confirming that the Shroud had spent time in these places. One is therefore forced to admit that the Shroud originally came from Palestine and Asia Minor.

A close connection was also discovered between the vegetable traces on the Shroud and some plants in biblical times. For example, the cap of thorns has been associated with the plant *Poterium spinosum*, a diagnosis which today is indirectly supported by the presence of its pollen on the Shroud as demonstrated by the Swiss criminologist Dr. Max Frei.

The Photographic Enigma

An extraordinary characteristic of the Shroud, photographically speaking, is its "negativity," that is, the imprints behave like a photographic negative (except for the blood stains, which are positive). In other words, they are dark, corresponding to the areas in relief of the man's body, and light elsewhere. Now, when we photograph something, we get a photographic negative on the film, that is, an image that presents light and shade completely reversed, and also a spatial transposition which changes right to left and vice versa. From the negative we then get photographs that reproduce the object as normally seen.

During the first exposition of the Shroud in 1898, the lawyer Secondo Pia was granted permission to photograph the Shroud. When developing the negative, he saw the features of a man appear in positive although it was a negative film. It was obvious to him that for a more immediate reading of the Shroud it was better to deal with the photographic negative, as, contrary to the norm, the image was much clearer.

The Carbon-dating Controversy

Now, carbon (C) contains six protons and it is present in nature as a mixture of three isotopes. Isotopes are atoms possessing nuclei with the same number of protons but with a different number of neutrons. Consequently, they are differentiated by atomic weight. The three isotopes of carbon present in all its compounds are represented by the following symbols; C_{12}, C_{13}, C_{14}. These figures identify the particular isotope by its atomic weight.

The atomic weight of an element indicates the sum of the protons and the neutrons in its nucleus. For example, carbon has an atomic weight of 6, but this weight can be 12, 13, or 14. This is because it can have 6, 7, or 8 neutrons in the nucleus besides the 6 protons. Now, while C_{12} and C_{13} are stable isotopes of carbon, C_{14} is unstable and hence it is radioactive. Its unstable nucleus is transformed by the emission of an electron into a nucleus of nitrogen. The speed at which radioactive decay takes place can be measured by counting the electron particles emitted by the system, and a simple way of visualizing this characteristic is expressed by the "half-life." This is the time necessary for the initial quantity of the radioisotope in question to be halved. With C_{14} the period of the "half-life" is equal to about 5730 years!

So said, a sample of the Shroud was taken in the sanctuary of the Turin Cathedral by a team of world scientists. It was removed from a single spot at the top left-hand corner of the Shroud. Three laboratories specializing in radiocarbon dating were each assigned one sample, weighing about 50 mg. The results were announced at a press conference on October 15, 1988. The Shroud had been carbon-dated to a period between 1260-1390 AD! Given this result, it was thought that the Shroud could not therefore be the sheet in which Christ's body had been wrapped when he was taken down from the Cross. This surprising and controversial dating of the sample of Shroud fabric would suggest, for example, that the Shroud was created by a medieval forger who, inspired by the Gospel to the letter, must have tortured and crucified someone in the Middle Ages for the very precise purpose of constructing a false winding sheet of Jesus. A hypothesis of this sort is totally unlikely, unscientific and unacceptable.

Scientists have now argued that textiles subjected to high temperatures for sufficiently long periods may fix carbon, resulting in a possible radiocarbon rejuvenation of the specimen. But dating by radiocarbon is also a very delicate method and requires complex calculations. It also requires corrective factors to be introduced in the calculations necessary for dating, depending on the material, on its state of preservation, on the periods it has spent in high temperatures, and by accidental contaminants.

As Dr. Thomas J. Phillips, of Harvard University's High Energy Physics Laboratory, commented: "If this Shroud of Turin is in fact the burial cloth of Christ ... then according to the Bible it was present at a unique physical event: the resurrection of a dead man. Unfortunately, that event is not accessible to direct scientific scrutiny, but ... the body may have radiated neutrons, which would have irradiated the Shroud and changed some of the nuclei to different isotopes by neutron capture. In particular, some carbon 14 could have been generated from carbon 13." In short, he is postulating that this extra carbon could possibly make the apparent age of the Shroud appear more recent than it really is.

More recently, Dr. Leoncio Garza-Valdes, a professor of microbiology of the University of Texas, USA, also discovered an organic "bioplastic coating" on the Shroud that had accumulated from the symbiotic activity of millions of bacteria and fungi, building up into a casing. Indeed, this bioplastic covering is probably related to the puzzling surface sheen noted on the Shroud. Dr. Garza-Valdes claims that this coating so distorted the carbon-dating process that the Shroud is actually significantly older than it was thought to be.

But there are several aspects to the Shroud which loudly testify that it is indeed the cloth of Christ. For example, on the man of the Shroud's head are wounds caused by a thorn-cap. This is something truly exceptional and there are no documents reporting any such head cap either among the Romans or other peoples. Moreover, after death the man of the Shroud was wrapped in a sheet. This was also something very uncommon in antiquity as in most cases the corpses of crucified men were left on the Cross itself, to be eaten by wild animals, or at best buried in a pauper's grave.

The evidence is that scarcely was the man of the Shroud down from the Cross when he was wrapped in a sheet without any washing or anointing of the corpse. This fact also does not tally with the custom of the time in which a normal burial involved the washing, anointing with spices, and clothing of the corpse. However, some spices, such as myrrh and aloes, were put on the sheet, as has been shown by the discovery of these substances on the Shroud. Evidently this is an exceptional case in which certain external factors intervened, leading to a hurried burial.

The recent discovery of the imprint of a coin on the left eye, discovered by Professor Filas and later confirmed by the researchers Tamburelli, Whanger, and Moroni, is a valid confirmation of a burial usage at the time of Christ. The type of coin itself has also been dated approximately to the first years of the Christian era. We may therefore conclude that the probability is extremely high that the man of the Shroud is Jesus of Nazareth.

And so, a wide margin of uncertainties, including the lack of precise knowledge of how cellulose textiles kept in historically non-controlled conditions react during the aging process, suggests a proper prudence in determining the age of the Shroud. The consideration of the above leads us to conclude that the results of these 1988 tests may be regarded as inconclusive. In fact, I do suspect that science would soon prove itself wrong and acknowledge that the Shroud of Turin is indeed the Shroud of Christ. It will certainly be all part of God's plan and timing.

As Dr. Pierre Barbet, the author of *A Doctor at Calvary*, said: "Science can do no more than keep silence, for the phenomenon is outside its domain. But for the man of learning at least there is proof of the resurrection." And so, the physical body, with its thorns and punctured flesh, has left a lingering testimony to scientists and faithful alike. It was a horrible mutilation. But will it help us to show more gratitude to the man on the Shroud for the suffering he endured for us?

Chapter 12

Gratitude and Ingratitude

"Now on the way to Jerusalem he travelled along the border between Samaria and Galilee. As he entered one of the villages, ten lepers came to meet him. They stood someway off and called to him, 'Jesus! Master! Take pity on us.' When he saw them he said, 'Go and show yourself to the priest.' Now as they were going away they were cleansed. Finding themselves cured, one of them turned back praising God at the top of his voice and threw himself at the feet of Jesus and thanked him. The man was a Samaritan. This made Jesus say, "Were not all ten made clean? The other nine, where are they? It seems as though no one has come back to give praise to God, except this foreigner" (Luke 17:11-19).

It is the Old Testament's example *par excellence* of ingratitude. One out of ten! It probably represents the true percentage of us creatures who show and express gratitude to the Creator. Indeed, ingratitude is an experience that few have not had. It greatly outweighs gratitude in the scale of human behaviour and expression. William Shakespeare put it into the mouth of Amiens in *As You Like It*: "Blow, blow, thou winter wind! Thou art not as unkind as man's ingratitude."

Returning kindness with unkindness, graciousness with ungraciousness, thoughtfulness with thoughtlessness; this is what ingratitude is all about. So common it is that one would have thought it was a commandment! It is the antonym of appreciation. Even Cyrano de Bergerac in "declining " an offer, did it graciously: "No, thank you. No, I thank you. And again I thank you."

In the diary of Sr. Maria Faustina Kowalska (1905-1938), that very privileged nun from Poland who had conversations with Our Lord in his role as the "Divine Mercy," she recorded in 1935 that Jesus said to her: "How indifferent are souls to so much goodness, to so many proofs of my love! My heart thinks only of the *ingratitude* and thoughtlessness of souls living in the world.... In return for my blessings, I get *ingratitude*. In return for my love, I get forgetfulness and indifference.... I am more deeply wounded by the small imperfections of chosen souls than by the sins of those living in the world. These little imperfections are not all. I will reveal to you a secret of my heart: what I suffer from chosen souls. Ingratitude on the part of such souls in return for so many graces is my heart's constant food. Their love is lukewarm, and my heart cannot bear it."

It was not a new complaint. In 1675, he lamented to St. Margaret Mary Alacoque in Paray le Monial, France: "Behold this heart which has so much love for men, that it spared nothing, even to exhausting and consuming itself, in order to give them testimony of its love. If only they would give me some return for my love, I would think but little of all that I have done for them and would wish, were it possible, to suffer still more. But in return I mostly receive only ingratitude through their irreverence and sacrileges, and through the coldness and scorn that they have for me in the Sacrament of Love. But what gives me most sorrow is that there are hearts consecrated to me who treat me thus. Do you at least console me by making up for the ingratitude as far as you can."

Jesus, himself gave thanks to the Father when he was on earth: "Then he instructed the crowd to sit on the ground, and he took the seven loaves, and after *giving thanks* he broke them and handed them to his disciples to distribute" (Mark 8:6). Then at the institution of the Eucharist, "he took some bread, and when he had *given thanks*, broke it and gave it to them, saying: "This is my body which will be given up for you; do this in memory of me." (Luke 32:19-20). But gratitude is not only the memory but the homage of the heart rendered to God for his goodness, and he, in turn, we can be assured, will graciously acknowledge, and say: "Thanks for the memory!" Indeed, heaven itself must be one big "Thank you." As Izaac Walton once said: "God has two dwellings; one in heaven, and the other in a meek and thankful heart."

Now, after supper on that Thursday night and during his anguish in the Garden of Gethsemane, as related by the mystic, stigmatist and visionary, the Venerable Anne Catherine Emmerich (1774-1824), a nun of the Order of St. Augustine in the convent in Westphalia in Germany, through the visions which she received on the life of Our Lord, wrote that he cried: "O my Father, can I possibly suffer for so *ungrateful* a people? O my Father, if this chalice may pass from me. But I must drink it. Thy will be done!"

But because of his *undying* love for us, he drank of the cup and *died* for us. He was murdered on the Cross because of our sins with which we are all so in love. As Louis of Granada (1604-1688) once anguished: "How can we look then with indifference on the murderers of Our Lord? And who are those murderers? None other than our sins. Our sins suspended him and bound him with fetters, landed him with infirmities, overwhelmed him with outrages, bruised him with blows, and nailed him to the Cross."

And so, our gratitude should excite us to praise him incessantly. As someone once said, gratitude is that inward feeling of kindness received. Thankfulness is the natural impulse to express that feeling. Thanksgiving is the sequel of that impulse. Thanksgiving, therefore, should be the first of all our religious commitments. It should introduce the beginning of all our days. Thanks for the day! Thanks for life! Thanks for the good times — and the bad times; we grew and learnt from them. Indeed, every day should be "Thanksgiving Day," for what else can we give to a God who needs nothing but to offer our thanks and our gratitude: "Give thanks to the Lord for he is good, his love is everlasting!" (Psalm 118:1).

But there has been no greater expression of thanks than that of the humble handmaid who exalted her Lord. It was an act of humble gratitude that he had chosen her, unworthy as she was, for an extraordinary favour — to be the "*Mother of the Lord*." It was Mary's song of thanksgiving: "My soul magnifies the Lord, and my spirit rejoices in God my saviour, for he has looked with favour on the lowliness of his servant...." (Luke 1:46-48). Gratitude is all that. It is a great and wonderful outpouring of the heart to the one who gives the gift. Gratitude is the very heart of love. And so, our daily prayer should be: "O Lord, you have given me so much, give me one thing more — a grateful heart. Amen."

Chapter 13

The First Marian Dogma – Mother of God

"And how does this happen to me that the mother of my Lord shall come to me," asks Elizabeth (Luke 1:43). Indeed, this is Mary's first and greatest privilege, the other privileges follow from this one. The biblical basis for this title, "Mother of my Lord," apart from Luke 1:43, is found in Matthew 1:23: "Behold the virgin shall be with child and bear a son, and they shall call him Emmanuel — a name which means 'God is with us.'" It is also in Luke 1:35: "And so, the child will be holy, and will be called Son of God," and in Galatians 4:4: "But when the appointed time came, God sent his son, born of woman." In short, Mary is indeed the Mother of God.

This title *Mother of God* was not rejected by anyone until 428 AD. On April 10, 428 AD, Nestorius, a priest of Antioch, was consecrated Bishop of Constantinople. He used the term Christokos (Mother of Christ) for Mary and not Theotokos (God bearer). The border lines were clearly drawn when one of his priests, Anastasius, whom he took with him from Antioch, preaching in December 428 AD, declared: "Let no one call Mary 'Theotokos,' for Mary was but a woman, and it is impossible that God should be born from a woman." This teaching Nestorius publicly approved and he himself preached.

However, the Church's earliest teaching, based on Scripture, was that Jesus was one person, fully human (Hebrew 2:14,17) and yet divine or "true God" (1 John 5:20). Now, since this one person was born of Mary, she is truly the mother of one divine person. And so, the one Jesus was both God and man, and he was referred to in each of these roles separately, as the "Son of God" and the "Son of man," at different times and in different contexts. In other words, in his divine nature he produced her but in his human nature he was produced by her. She was not the mother of the divinity of Jesus, but the mother of the divine person, Jesus. She was neither the mother of his human nature. Motherhood relates to the *person* of the offspring, not the *nature*. In short, your mother is not the mother of your human nature, but of you, the person.

With this distinction, we can thus say that in one role he created Mary and in another he was procreated by her, that is to say, in his divine nature he produced her but in his human nature he was produced by her. She was not the mother of the humanity of Jesus, but the mother of the human person. She was also not the mother of the divinity of Jesus, but the mother of the divine person, Jesus. Motherhood relates to the *person* of the offspring, not the *nature*. In short, your mother is not the mother of your human nature, but of you, the person.

But how can God have a mother, some critics ask, since that would imply that she is older than God? Sure, they say, she was only Christ's mother, all in an effort to escape honouring Mary. However, as divine, the second Person of the Trinity had *no beginning*, but an eternal past. Yet as human, he had a beginning *in time* in the womb of Mary. Indeed, that same Jesus claimed that he had existed before Abraham. "Before Abraham was I am" (John 8:58), and even before the world (John 17:5). All this proves that Jesus is one person with two natures, one without a beginning, one with a beginning. Obviously, Mary did not exist before God. Jesus is the Son of God from all *eternity,* who became also the Son of Mary in *time.* And so, whereas she gave him his flesh and blood, his divinity was given by the Father. The one Jesus was therefore both God and man.

On June 22, 431 AD, the third ecumenical Council was held at Ephesus, over which St. Cyril presided. Nestorius was deposed and excommunicated, his Christological doctrine was condemned and the title "Theotokos," Mother of God, solemnly recognized. The decision taken at Ephesus was explicitly promulgated as dogma in 451 AD by the Council of Chalcedon. The controversy did not surface again in Christianity until some time *after* the Reformation. But the three great pillars of the Reformation, Luther, Calvin and Zwingli, all accepted this doctrine wholeheartedly. Indeed, most Protestants have been surprised when told that although the founders of Protestantism rejected many Catholic doctrines, they actually insisted on honouring Mary as Mother of God.

For example, in 1539, Luther wrote in a treatise entitled *Of Councils and Churches*: "Hence this Council (of Ephesus) did not establish anything new in the faith, but defended the ancient faith against the new vagueness of Nestorius. Indeed, the article according to which Mary is Mother of God has been in the Church from the beginning and has not been newly produced by the Council but on the contrary is contained in the Gospel and in the Holy Scripture ..."(Martin Luther's works, Weimar, 50:591,22-592). Huldrych Zwingli, the Swiss Reformer, also wrote in 1524: "I have never thought, still less taught, or declared publicly, anything concerning the subject of the ever Virgin Mary, mother of our salvation, which could be considered dishonourable, impious, unworthy or evil.... I hope this is sufficient to have made plain to pious and simple Christians my clear conviction on the matter of the Mother of God. I believe with all my heart according to the word of the holy gospel that this pure Virgin bore for us the Son of God and that she remained, in the birth and after it, a pure and unsullied virgin for eternity" (Von der ewig reinen Magd. Maria, der Mutter Gottes, Huldrych Zwingli, Collected Works, Berlin, 1,391-428).

Timothy Ware, an Orthodox priest, once spoke of the similarity between the Roman Catholic Church and the Orthodox Church with respect to Mary as Mother of God. He said: "Orthodox, like Roman Catholics, venerate the Mother of God but in no sense do the members of either Church regard her as a fourth person of the Trinity nor do they assign to her the worship due to God alone.... We honour Mary because she is the Mother of God. We do not venerate her in isolation but because of her relation to Christ. But the maternal rights exercised by Mary over her Son are much more of a privilege than a right, and the authority which she has over Jesus is only an authority conceded to her out of his goodness, kindness, love and humility. As Son of God, begotten from all eternity, Jesus does not and cannot depend on any creature, not even his mother, but in his human nature he is the servant of his father and subject to the authority of his mother." And so, according to St. Eiphanus of Salamis in Cyprus, may I add: "Let Mary be honoured, but let the Lord be worshipped."

Chatper 14

The Second Marian Dogma – The Perpetual Virginity of Mary

In 649 AD, the Lateran Council defined the second Marian dogma — the Perpetual Virginity of the Blessed Virgin Mary. While hardly any Catholic challenges the doctrine of Mary's virginity and the miraculous virgin birth of Jesus since it is clearly detailed in Matthew 1:18-25, affirmed by Luke 1:27, stated by Mary herself (Luke 1:34), and acknowledged by the archangel Gabriel (Luke 1:35-37), there are those who still debate the doctrine of Mary's *perpetual virginity* out of an unfortunate lack of knowledge of the Bible, or a deliberate obstinacy in not wishing to acknowledge the truth in their prejudiced commitment to dishonour *"the Mother of the Lord."*

In calling Mary "ever virgin," Catholic and Orthodox tradition is saying that after conceiving Jesus in virginity, Mary always remained a virgin, abstaining from all conjugal relations. It also implies that the birth of Jesus left intact the virginity of his mother. On the other hand, when Protestants use the term the Virgin Mary, they mean that she was a virgin only *until* the birth of Jesus. They believe that she later had children, all those called "the brethren of the Lord" in the Bible.

Now, the Hebrew and Aramaic language spoken by Christ and his disciples do not have two separate words for "brother," "cousin," or "near-relative." For example, in the original Hebrew translation, Lot is called "Abraham's brother" (Genesis 14:14). Yet we know that Lot was Abraham's nephew (Genesis 11:27). Indeed, the Jews used the word "brother" for any near-relative, without necessarily meaning "sibling." From the fourth century, almost all great religious teachers agreed with the statements of the Second Council of Constantinople (353 AD) regarding Mary's perpetual virginity. All these brilliant scholars knew that the Greek words for "brothers and sisters" were also used to refer to other close relatives — cousins, nephews, nieces, et cetera.

But this is the custom even in some parts of modern-day Africa. In his book *The Long Walk to Freedom — The Autobiography of Nelson Mandela,* he wrote: "In African culture the sons and daughters of one's aunts or uncles are considered brothers and sisters, not cousins. We do not make the same distinction among relatives as practiced by whites. We have no half-brothers or half-sisters. My mother's sister is my mother. My uncle's son is my brother. My brother's child is my son, my daughter."

Moreover, in the Scriptures Mary is never called the mother of these "brothers of the Lord." There is also no mention of them in the episode of the three days' loss of Jesus at the age of twelve, yet it would have been unthinkable for a Jewish mother to leave her other children at home so that she might travel for this great feast in Jerusalem. Nor would Mary have been consigned to the care of John by Jesus on Calvary (John 19:27) if there were close siblings who could and should take care of her. All of this, and much more circumstantial evidence, confirm that the "brothers and sisters" of Jesus were kinsfolk but not siblings, thus indirectly supporting the ancient tradition of Mary's continued virginity after the birth of Jesus.

The womb that bore the God Incarnate was exclusively reserved for him alone. In fact, God also saw it fit to highlight his Son's divinity by a certain exclusivity in several aspects of his life. For instance, in manifesting his palm-strewn entrance into Jerusalem, Jesus chose to ride on a colt that *no one* had ever ridden (Luke 19:30). He was laid in a tomb that *no one* had been laid in before (John 19:41). And so, he chose the womb of a virgin who had never known man, and who would bear *no one* but himself. This sacred vessel, therefore, that bore the Messiah was to be reserved for him alone. How else could it have been! It was the Tabernacle of the Most High.

Theologians also believe that this was foretold in the Old Testament passage in Ezekiel 44:2-3: "This gate shall remain shut, for the Lord, the God of Israel, has entered it. The Prince himself is the only one who sits inside the gateway." It is noteworthy that this was the eastern gate about which Ezekiel spoke, and is the one that led directly to the sanctuary of the temple, for "the glory of the Lord entered the temple through the gate facing east" (Ezekel 40:6). Significantly, this Eastern Golden Gate of Jerusalem is still closed to this day!

But the fundamentalists also argue their point on the verse: "And he knew her not *till* she brought forth her first-born son" (Matthew 1:25). They argue that the natural inference from "till" is that Joseph and Mary lived together afterwards as husband and wife in the usual sense, and had several children. But *"until"* or *"till"* in the Bible simply means that "something" did not happen up to a certain point. It certainly does not imply that the something did happen later, which is the modern sense of the term.

In fact, if the modern sense of the word is forced on the Bible, some ridiculous meanings result. Consider this line, for example: "Michal, the daughter of Saul, had no children *until* the day of her death" (2 Samuel 6:23). Are we, therefore, to assume that she had children *after* her death? Then there was the burial of Moses. About the location of his grave, it was said that "no man knows, *until* this present day" (Deuteronomy 34:6). But we do know that no one has known since that day either.

These examples could be multiplied. In short, it should be clear that nothing at all can be proved from the use of the word *"till"* in Matthew 1:25. Recent translations give a better sense of the verse: "He had no relations with her at any time before she bore a son" (New American Bible) and: "He had not known her when she bore a son" (Knox translation).

They also ask, bringing up their second point, why then would Jesus be called first-born? Does this not mean that there must have been a "second born," etc? However, under the Mosaic Law, it was the "first-born" son that was to be sanctified (Exodus 34:20). To the first-born came the birthright. And so, the first male child of a marriage was termed the "first-born" *even if* he turned out to be the only child of the marriage. This usage is aptly illustrated by a funerary inscription discovered in Egypt. The inscription refers to a woman who died during the birth of her "first-born"!

At the time of the Annunciation the Scripture says: "She was found to be with child through the Holy Spirit" (Matthew 1:18-19). "She has conceived what is in her by the Holy Spirit" (Matthew 1:21). "The Holy Spirit will come upon you," the angel answered, "and the power of the Most High will cover you with its shadow. And so, the child will be holy and will be called the son of God" (Luke 1:35-36). This daughter of the Father then became the bride of the Holy Spirit. For this bride therefore to have any intimate relationship with the foster-father of Jesus would be against the fourth commandment: "Thou shalt not commit adultery." And so, she was perpetually a virgin. It is not only theological sense. It is more basic than that. It is common sense.

But it also seems that today's Protestants and all those others who protest against Mary's perpetual virginity do not also know this history of their Protestantism, for in this also the founders of their own Protestant tradition strongly supported the perpetual virginity of Mary. This is what Luther had to say: "It is an article of faith that Mary is Mother of the Lord and still a virgin.... Christ, we believe, came forth from a womb left perfectly intact" (*Works of Luther*, v.11,319-320; v.6,510).

Calvin was no less supportive: "There have been certain folk who have wished to suggest from this passage (Matthew 1:25) that the Virgin Mary had other children other than the Son of God and that Joseph had then dwelt with her later; but what folly this is! For the Gospel writer did not wish to record what happened afterwards: he simply wished to make clear Joseph's obedience and to show that Joseph had been well and truly assured that it was God who had sent his angel to Mary. He had therefore never dwelt with her nor had he shared her company.... And besides this, Our Lord Jesus Christ is called the first-born. This is not because there was a second or a third, but because the Gospel writer is paying regard to the precedence. Scripture speaks thus of naming the first-born whether or not there was any question of the second" (Calvin, *Sermon on Matthew* 1:22-25, published in 1562).

The Swiss Reformer Zwingli was equally assertive: "I firmly believe that Mary, according to the words of the Gospel, was a pure Virgin and brought forth for us the Son of God and in child-birth and after childbirth was forever a pure, intact Virgin" (Zwingli, Opera, v.1,424). She would personally confirm this in years to come when she appeared in Guadalupe, Mexico, to Juan Diego in 1531.

Chapter 15

Santa Maria de Guadalupe of Spain

It appears that St. Luke, apart from being a physician, was a great artist and sculptor (the icon of Our Lady of Perpetual Help is credited to him). He is alleged to have sculptured a statue of Our Lady. Ancient manuscripts suggest that when the evangelist died in Acaya (Asia Minor), buried with him was his statue of Our Lady. When his remains were removed to Constantinople in the mid-fourth century, the image was taken to Rome by Cardinal Gregorio, who had been living in Constantinople as legate to Pope Pelaguis II (579–590 AD).

In the year 590 AD, Gregorio Magno (Gregory the Great) was elected Pope (590–604 AD). He was so devoted to the statue that he exhibited it in his oratory. The Pope eventually sent it as a present of goodwill to San Leandro, Archbishop of Seville, Spain, who then had it enthroned in the main church where it was venerated until the beginning of the Moorish invasion in 711 AD. Towards 714 AD, some clergymen who were fleeing from the Moorish peril brought with them the statue, which they hid in the banks of the River Guadalupe.

Six centuries later, in 1326, there was great joy among the people when a shepherd named Gil Cordero related that while he was searching for a lost cow he found the entrance to an underground cave and there was the statue of unstained wood with its pertinent documents. Although it had been hidden for six hundred years, it was in perfect condition. It was considered to be a symbol of the Virgin's "royal maternity" since the statue holds in its left hand the Child Jesus while the right hand clasps a scepter. A chapel was later built there by the order of King Alfonso XI (1312-50 AD) and the statue enthroned therein was named *Santa Maria de Guadalupe* after the village located near the place of discovery. Guadalupe (which means hidden river) is situated in the Altamira hills in Extremadura. The River Guadalupe irrigates its fields.

With great pomp and ceremony, the king visited the chapel in 1340, fourteen years after the statue's discovery. Queen Isabel and King Ferdinand of Spain were also staunch devotees of the Shrine of *Our Lady of Guadalupe* and made many pilgrimages there. Indeed, the popularity of the shrine was at its height during the time of the great discoveries of Christopher Columbus, who reportedly carried a replica of the statue with him as, so it is said, did Hernan Cortes and some of the other later conquistadors.

It is also believed that Columbus prayed at the shrine before making his historic voyage. In fact, during his second voyage, upon discovering the West Indies' island of Karukere on November 4, 1493, he renamed it *Santa Maria de Guadalupe* in honour of the Blessed Virgin, now the French island of Guadeloupe in the Caribbean.

The shrine of *Our Lady of Guadalupe* is now located in the church within the fortress-like Monastery of Guadalupe, and the statue can be seen behind the main altar in an ornate and richly decorated panelled wall. The monastery is now in the care of the Franciscans and is still frequently visited by pilgrims, both local and foreign. On October 12, 1928, *Our Lady of Guadalupe* was "crowned" as Queen of all the Hispanidad by the Primate Cardinal Don Pedro Segura, special legate to Pope Pius XI. The sanctuary was elevated in 1955 to the honour of Cathedral by Pope Pius XII and was honoured by Pope John Paul II by his visit there in 1982.

My first visit to the sanctuary was on Sunday, March 14, 1999. It was a four-hour coach journey from Madrid. Behind the main altar, the cubicle containing the statue of *Our Lady of Guadalupe*, dressed in traditional Spanish garb, was readily seen. The cubicle in which it is placed was brightly lit in comparison to the other panels. This image of *Our Lady of Guadalupe* would in time play a very important role in the evangelization of the New World by Columbus and later by Cortes.

Chapter 16

Christianity Sails to the New World

She was called Isabel the Catholic and was the greatest woman ruler in all history, one of the supreme champions of the Roman Catholic Faith in the 15th century. She, like most Spaniards at the time, had a great devotion to the Blessed Virgin Mary and frequently visited the shrine of Santa Maria de Guadalupe (Holy Mary of Guadalupe) in Extremadura, Spain. In fact she spent her 35th birthday at the shrine and also stayed there for two weeks in the month of June 1492, the year of Columbus' first voyage to the Indies.

Seven hundred and forty years before Isabel (1451–1504) was born, an utterly alien army had landed by the Rock of Gibraltar near the southern tip of Spain. They spoke a language, Arabic, never before heard in Spain. They proclaimed the faith of Muhammad the prophet, called Islam, affirming God but rejecting Christ as the Son of God. The goal of their militant crusade was the conquest of the world, and by the year 711AD they were close to achieving it. Unprepared and overwhelmed, the Christian kingdom of Spain disintegrated before the invaders in just three years.

It was not until 1492 with the fall of Granada that the long Islamic domination of as long as 770 years ended in triumph for Catholic Spain. It was in that same year that Isabel made a final decision to sponsor Columbus in an enterprise in search of the Indies, in which she was belatedly but fully supported by King Ferdinand. In fact, this adventure made Isabel's Spain the world's greatest power for a century and a half, and the saviour of Catholic Europe, thanks to a Genoese sailor who was called in Spanish Cristobál Colón and signed his name in Latin, Christopher Columbus.

When Columbus was born, Europe, Africa, and Asia were each part of the Old World of the Eastern Hemisphere, but they were separate worlds culturally, religiously and politically. The world of the Western Hemisphere, on the other hand, stood completely apart and isolated from the Old World as it had been for thousands of years. Deeply influenced by millenarian and apocalyptic visionaries, one of his professed goals was to hasten the conversion of the world to Christianity, and as early as his first voyage, he suggested that all profits from his enterprise should be used for the Christian re-conquest of Jerusalem from the Muslims. It is also said that Columbus made a pilgrimage to the shrine of Santa Maria de Guadalupe in Extremadura before he began his journey in search of the Indies.

He set sail from Palos in Spain in the three most famous ships in history with sails emblazoned with large red crosses. The *Santa Clara* was named after St. Clare, the first Franciscan nun and a close friend of St. Francis of Assisi, the founder of the Order. The ship was also nicknamed *Niña* (little girl). The other two ships were the *Pinta* (from *pintar,* meaning to paint) and the *Santa Maria,* the flag ship and the largest of the fleet. It carried about forty men.

The day selected for departure reflected the profound Catholic faith of the people from whom Columbus' crew was drawn. August 2, 1492 was at that time the feast of Our Lady of the Angels, patroness of the Franciscan monastery of La Rábida. In fact, Columbus, like Queen Isabel, was a Third Order lay Franciscan. Indeed, he scheduled his departure for the day following the feast so that his men could join in thanksgiving and prayer with their families on that feast day especially dear to them.

The next morning, Friday, August 3, Columbus' three ships weighed anchor and sailed down the shallow bay. Out in the midst of the Atlantic, the ships were making a world-historic crossing, and every evening at 5:00 p.m. the whole crew sang the *Salve Regina* (Hail, Holy Queen), a petition-prayer to the Blessed Virgin Mary.

"Hail, Holy Queen, Mother of mercy, our life, our sweetness and our hope. To you do we cry, poor banished children of Eve, to you do we send our sighs, mourning and weeping in this valley of tears. Turn then, most gracious Advocate, your eyes of mercy towards us, and after this our exile, show unto us the blessed fruit of your womb, Jesus. O clement, O loving, O sweet Virgin Mary."

In the thirteenth century, the great Marian prayer *Sub Tuum* was added to the litany of Marian prayers to the Blessed Virgin Mary:

"We fly to your patronage, O holy Mother of God. Despise not our petitions in our necessities, but deliver us always from all dangers, O glorious and blessed Virgin."

By October 1, they had crossed more than 2,000 miles, but not seeing land for so long a time caused such dismay that the men of the *Santa Maria* were on the verge of open mutiny. However, at 2:00 a.m. on October 12, land was sighted at last. It was on the great Spanish feast day of *El Pilar,* the Virgin of Saragossa, and the first Marian shrine in Spain. Coincidence? Hardly! Did not Einstein say, "God does not play dice!"

At dawn Columbus and the two other captains went ashore in the *Santa Maria's* launch. They unfolded the banner of Isabel and Ferdinand, displaying a large green cross and the letters F and Y (sometimes "Ysabel" was used instead of Isabel), each surmounted by a crown on the left and right sides of the cross. It was an island in the Bahamian chain of isles which was previously called in the native tongue, Guanahani. Columbus then took possession of the island for Isabel and Ferdinand and the Spain they ruled, and renamed it San Salvador, after the Saviour.

Soon afterwards, the natives began to appear, naked except for loincloths, brown-skinned, wondering but friendly. It was the first meeting of the Old and the New World *nations*. Columbus was struck by the skin colour of the islanders. Assuming that he was near India, he called them Indians, noting that they were not as dark-skinned as Africans, but rather the colour of the Canary Islanders.

Now, I was fortunate to obtain a copy of Columbus' diary, and in it I observed that on Monday, November 12, 1492, he wrote: "These people have no religious beliefs, nor are they idolaters. They are very gentle and do not know what evil is; nor do they kill others, nor steal (he would later discover that some of the Carib tribes were cannibals and violent); and they are without weapons and so timid that a hundred of them flee from one of our men even if our men are teasing them. They are credulous and aware that there is a God in heaven and are convinced that we come from the heavens, and they say very quickly any prayer that we tell them to say, and they make the sign of the cross. So that your Highnesses ought to resolve to make them Christians: for I believe that if you begin, in a short time you will end up having converted to our Holy Faith a multitude of peoples and acquiring large dominions and great riches and all of their peoples for Spain."

Before sailing from San Salvador, Columbus asked his Indian informants about nearby islands. The fleet then took possession of an island on October 16, giving it the name of Santa Maria de la Concepción. In short, it was a dedication firstly to Our Saviour (San Salvador) and then to Our Lady (Santa Maria de la Concepción). Proper protocol. *Santa Maria* was the flag ship and so, one may well say that it was an example of St. Louis de Montfort's religious slogan: "To Jesus through Mary."

About ten in the morning, the fleet departed for yet another island, which Columbus named Fernandina after King Ferdinand, and on Friday October 19, he reached an island which the "Indians" called Samoet, to which he gave the new name, Isabel. He eventually discovered Cuba and then a larger island called Babeque which he would later rename Hispaniola, and which today is divided into Haiti and the Dominican Republic.

However, the auspicious beginning of Columbus' stay on Hispaniola was spoilt when disaster struck the fleet between Haiti and the Dominican Republic on Christmas Eve. The *Santa Maria* went aground on a bank off the northern coast of the island. Columbus then abandoned his flagship and took his crew to the *Niña*.

I must confess, however, that I was most surprised that the *Santa Maria*, the flagship dedicated to the Virgin Mary, was shipwrecked!

On their return journey to Spain, on February 12, the ships sailed into one of the most terrible storms ever experienced. For six hours the ordeal continued with no signs of relief. Columbus then called his men together and they vowed to make a pilgrimage to the great shrine of Santa Maria de Guadalupe in Spain if they were spared, with their representative to be chosen by lot. This lot fell to Columbus.

After sunset on the 14th, the skies began to clear and the next morning an island was sighted in the Azores, previously discovered and settled by Portugal. The fishermen there could not imagine how the little ship they saw sailing in had escaped the fury of the tempest. I could not but think that the haven found following the tempest was not a coincidence. It was an island named *Santa Maria*! I well understood its providential and prophetic significance.

On March 15, Columbus sailed into Palos from where he had departed seven and a half months before. About an hour or two later the *Pinta* soon followed the *Niña*. The next day was Palm Sunday and the Admiral spent Holy Week in Seville with ten Indian captives he had brought with him. He had come to Holy Week in Seville, above all to give thanks to God through participating in the glorious pageantry commemorating the death and resurrection of Christ, and which still commands the attendance of thousands of Catholics throughout Spain (indeed, in June 1990, I was present at that impressive Good Friday procession around the Cathedral of Seville, the third largest church in the Christian world). The ten Indians Columbus had brought with him were later baptized, with Isabel and Ferdinand as their sponsors. He then went to the shrine of Santa Maria de Guadalupe in Extremadura, fulfilling his vow taken during the great storm of the return voyage.

Arriving back in Seville, Columbus began engaging men for his second voyage (1493–96), and on September 25, 1493, he set sail once again for the Americas with a fleet of seventeen ships and some fifteen hundred men. Departing from the new royal port, Cádiz, the fleet included *Colina, La Gallega,* and a new flag ship *Santa Maria,* nicknamed *Mariagalante* (not, of course, the *Santa Maria* that had been wrecked off Hispaniola on the first voyage).

He set his course west by south and eventually sighted two islands on November 3. The first he named Dominica, after the Latin word for "Lord God," and the second he called Santa Maria la Galante for his flagship. Later, on November 4, he discovered an island named Karukere and re-named it Santa Maria de Guadalupe after the Virgin of Guadalupe in Spain (this island is now called Guadeloupe in French since the French conquest of the island in 1635). After leaving Guadalupe, the fleet sailed north and they discovered what is called the Leeward Islands, and gave some names for the Virgin Mary and others for the saints, including one of his own names, San Cristobal (St. Christopher), now St. Kitts. Among them were the Marian names Santa Maria de Montserrat and Santa Maria la Antigua (now simply called Montserrat and Antigua since Spain lost its colonies in the Caribbean).

On May 30, 1498, the third voyage began with eight ships, and on July 31, he reached an island off the northeastern coast of South America and because he saw from afar three close mountain peaks, he called the island La Trinidad in honour of the Trinity. The fleet anchored and he sent a party ashore at what is now called Erin Bay in Trinidad. On further exploration, the fleet reached the mouth of the impressive Orinoco River. Columbus actually thought that he was near Paradise or somewhere like it. As he said in his diary: "I have never read or heard of so great a quantity of fresh water ... and if it does not come from there, from Paradise, it seems to be a still greater marvel, for I do not believe that there is known in the world a river so great and so deep." He had discovered Venezuela and the southern continent of America.

Columbus died in Valladolid in 1506, still believing that he was close to Asia, but he had discovered a New World unknown to Europeans. During the 16th century, pirates sailed to the Caribbean almost continuously from ports in Western England and Northern France. All sought booty. Many were also strong and avowed Protestants, who added hatred of the Catholic Spanish to their lust for loot. And so, the sailors of these other nations began to attack Spain's treasure fleet and the Caribbean colonies, and until the final collapse of Spanish power in the 1670s and 1680s, Spanish ships and ports provided the main prey for pirates in the Caribbean and some of the islands became colonies of France, Britain and the Netherlands.

Four centuries after Columbus' discoveries, Pope Leo XIII (1878–1903), in his encyclical *Quarto Abrupto Soeculo* of July 16, 1902, paid tribute to him and said that in a letter to Pope Alexander VI (1492–1503), Columbus had written: "I trust that by God's help I may spread the Holy Name and Gospel of Jesus Christ as widely as may be." Pope Leo mentioned elsewhere in his encyclical that "at each disembarkation he offered prayers to Almighty God, nor did he take possession save 'in the name of Jesus Christ.' Upon whatever shores he might be driven, his first act was to set upon the shore the standard of the Holy Cross." The Pope also quoted Columbus as saying that he "sought nothing from his enterprise and endeavour but the increase and the glory of the Christian religion."

Leo XIII spoke no ill of Columbus, but present-day historians highlight the fact that a journey which began in 1492 for God, glory and gold had by the second voyage onwards reversed its priority, and among the other failings of Columbus, he unashamedly waged war against the native inhabitants of the Caribbean and enslaved hundreds of them, hoping to profit from a transatlantic slave trade. In so doing, he angered the Spanish Crown by waging war and taking slaves in direct contravention of the royal order.

Nonetheless, whatever his faults, he spearheaded one of the greatest events in Church and world history. Moreover, he brought Christianity and devotion to the Blessed Virgin Mary to the Caribbean (named after the Carib indians) and the Americas. He found the Americas at a time when a great storm was raging throughout the Church in Europe after Martin Luther started a Reformation which resulted in the loss of millions from the Catholic faith. The loss in numbers was replenished in the New World, first by Columbus and then by Cortes and others.

Chapter 17

From Cortes to Mary

Columbus died in 1506, and in 1519 a Spanish expedition left from Cuba under the leadership of Hernan Cortes, who, as fate would have it, was from Extremadura, Spain. But I did say that God does not play dice! The original plan for Cortes' expedition to Mexico, as conceded by the governor of Cuba who had authorized it, was to seek gold and slaves, not conquest or settlement. However, marching inland from Veracruz on the Mexican coast, the expedition met many tribes who resented Aztec power. The Tlaxcalans and some of their neighbours were therefore pleased to welcome the newcomers, hoping to use them in their own struggle against the dreaded and seemingly all-powerful Aztecs. And so the Spaniards formed alliances with the Aztecs' enemies even before their initial contact with them.

The empire of the Aztecs was ruled at that time by Moctezuma II, and nowhere in world history had Satan so formalized his cult as in the Aztec empire at that time. Nowhere in known history had human sacrifices been performed on such a massive scale, and over 50,000 sacrifices were made annually as the hearts of their captive victims were plucked out of their chests while still alive as offerings to the pagan sun god, Huitzilopochtli. After a long, brutal, and bloody siege, on August 13, 1521, the Aztec capital city Tenochtitlan fell to the Spaniards. Following the conquest of the Aztec empire, their whole kingdom was then called New Spain and Tenochtitlan was given the name Mexico City. It was two years after Cortes landed on Veracruz.

Now, in the Spanish imperial system, conversion to Christianity was an essential complement to conquest, and so, conquering and colonizing ventures were as much missionary endeavours as military ones. With the subsequent arrival of the Franciscans, Dominicans, and later the Augustinian priests from Spain, conversions were frequent but there were many pockets of resistance, that is to say, until the year 1531. On Saturday, December 9, 1531, Her Majesty the Blessed Virgin appeared on the hill of Tepeyac outside Mexico City to an Aztec convert named Juan Diego, and after identifying herself to him, she sent him to the bishop of Mexico, the Franciscan Juan de Zumarraga, with instructions to have a church built on that site in her honour. Tepeyac hill was previously the site of the temple of the pagan Aztec mother-goddess Tonantzin. The Aztecs were to have a new mother, the Mother of the true God and the Mother of all Nations.

Not unexpectedly, the bishop was skeptical of Juan Diego's message and asked for a sign to confirm it. In response the Virgin had Juan Diego return to the top of the hill where this time he found a garden of beautiful Spanish Castilian roses (not yet introduced into Mexico) blooming out of season in a terrain where they could not ordinarily grow. He took the flowers to the Virgin, who arranged them herself in his tilma (cloak) and he then carried them to the bishop. When he unfolded the tilma in the bishop's presence, the roses cascaded to the floor and, to the added astonishment of all, the miraculous portrait of the Virgin was seen on the tilma. Asking forgiveness for his skepticism, the bishop knelt before the image and immediately undertook the order for the construction of a small chapel on Tepeyac hill. Juan Diego was appointed custodian of the chapel and the tilma, which was on display in it. It is said that when he was alone with the image (but secretly watched by others), he was often seen talking to it.

The image of the Virgin on the tilma is the great masterpiece of artistic facial expression and bodily contour, but to the Aztec Indians it was much more than a mere portrait. It was a pictograph which they were able to read and understand. The lady standing on the moon in front of and brighter than the sun signified that she was greater than their dreaded sun god Huitzilopochtli. The turquoise blue of her mantle, trimmed with gold, and the rose colour of her gown were the colours worn by Aztec royalty, and so, she was a queen. The stars strewn across her mantle confirmed to them that she was a celestial queen, yet she could not be a god since her head was slightly bowed in reverence and her hands were joined in prayer, obviously to One greater than herself.

The black cross on the gold brooch around her neck was identical to the cross on the banners and helmets of the Spanish Christian conquerors, telling them that her religion was that of the Spaniards. The sash around her waist with tassels signified that she was pregnant. In short, the miraculous image was a symbol of her "royal maternity" as was the statue of Santa Maria de Guadalupe in Spain. It was no coincidence! The Aztec land was called New Spain, and the Virgin came as the Spanish Santa Maria de Guadalupe of the New World. We call her Our Lady of Guadalupe.

But to the Christians the image meant much more. To them it was also a depiction of the woman of Revelation 11:19;12:1: "And the temple of God in heaven opened, and the ark of the covenant could be seen within it.... And a great sign appeared in heaven, a woman adorned with the sun, standing on the moon, and with twelve stars on her head for a crown." This is the same woman of Genesis 3:15, the woman whom the Church understands to be the Mother of the Saviour, conceived without the stain of original sin, and therefore worthy to be the Ark of the Covenant. It was the identical image that Satan was shown in heaven before his fall (see chapter 3).

The Verdict of Science

I will not go into the details of the miraculous aspects of the "painting" on the tilma as I have already done so in the book *A Scientist Researches Mary Mother and Co-Redemptrix*. Suffice it to say that modern scientific technology continues to confirm even more strongly than ever its miraculous origin. As Professor Callahan of the University of Florida once said: "It may seem strange for a scientist to say this, but as far as I am concerned, the original picture is miraculous.... Studying the image was the most moving experience of my life. Just getting that close I got the same strange feeling that the others who worked on the Shroud of Turin did. I believe in logical explanations up to a point. But there is no logical explanation to life. You can break life down into atoms, but what comes after that? Even Einstein said: 'God.' "

Referring to the miraculous tilma, Pope Benedict XIV (1724–30), after seeing a copy of it, quoted Psalm 147:20: "He has not done this for any other nation." Indeed, the tilma of Juan Diego can be compared to and associated with the Shroud of Christ, which is still believed to be the authentic burial cloth of her Son. In the tilma, the Virgin is pregnant with Christ. The Shroud is the cloth of the death and burial of Christ. One may therefore say that these two miraculous images, the one now in Turin, Italy, and the other in Mexico City, depict the story of Christ and his mother "from the womb to the tomb." They are depictions of the Redeemer and the Co-Redemptrix from Nazareth to Calvary.

Chapter 18

The Mother of All Mankind in Guadalupe, Mexico

But let us now discuss and analyze the words of the Virgin of Guadalupe when she introduced herself to Juan Diego. It was a statement which to me is the Marian anthem of anthems from the lips of the Queen herself:

> *"Know for certain, dearest of my sons, that I am the perfect and perpetual Virgin Mary, mother of the true God, through whom everything lives, the Lord of all things, who is master of heaven and earth. I ardently desire a temple be built here for me where I will show and offer my love, my compassion, my help and my protection to the people. I am your merciful mother; the mother of all who live united in this land, and of all mankind, and of all those who love me, of those who cry to me, of those who have confidence in me. Here, I will hear their weeping and their sorrows and will remedy and alleviate their sufferings, necessities and misfortunes."*

> *"I am the perfect and perpetual ever Virgin Mary, mother of the true God."*

See how in this one sentence she confirmed and ratified the first Marian dogma of Ephesus in 431 AD — Mother of God

(*Theotokos*) — and the second Marian dogma of the Lateran Council in 649 AD — the Perpetual Virginity of Mary! Moreover, by appearing on the feast of the Immaculate Conception, which at that time in Mexico was celebrated on December 9, 1531, she also gave us the first hint of the third Marian dogma — the Immaculate Conception. It was on a Saturday, the day traditionally dedicated to the Blessed Virgin Mary. See again how purposeful are her pronouncements in her private apparitions!

"I am your merciful mother."

Now, in the account of the alleged revelations given to St. Bridget of Sweden (1303–1373) by the Blessed Virgin Mary, an account considered by the Church to be worthy of belief if only because of the holiness and truthfulness of this great saint, the Virgin is claimed to have said to her: "I am called by all *Mother of Mercy*, and truly the mercy of my Son has made me merciful; and he is miserable, who will not, when he can, approach mercy" (St. Bridget in *Revl. lib 2c 23*). It is also written that she once heard Christ pressing his mother to ask some favour of him, assuring her that whoever should ask mercy through her should obtain it (St. Bridget in *Revl. lib 7.cap.10*). It is in this context that she is sometimes called *Mother of Mercy*.

In his Encyclical *Dives in Misericordia* (On God's Mercy), Pope John Paul II stated that "Mary is also the one who bestowed mercy in a particular and exceptional way, as no other person has … She is the one who has the deepest knowledge of the mystery of God's mercy. She knows its price. She knows how great it is. In this sense we call her the Mother of Mercy. The whole work of Redemption was an act of divine mercy, and God's mercy-made flesh, was incarnated in her."

"Mother of all who live united in this land...."

"Mother of all those who live united in this land," she said. Indeed, she has also been called *Mother of Unity*. After all, she is the mother of Jesus who cried in the Garden of Gethsemane on that night before his crucifixion: "I do pray …that they may all be one, even as you, Father, are in me and I in you…, that they may be one even as we are one" (John 17:20-22). It is particularly in this sense that she is the mother of all who live united (in one faith) on this earth.

"Mother … of all Mankind"

Here for the first time, at the beginning of her evangelization in the New World, she identifies herself as the *"Mother of all Mankind."* In other words, the *Mother of all Peoples* or the *Mother of all Nations.* This was four centuries before her Amsterdam apparitions!

The sequence of her statement "Mother of all who live united in this land," followed by "and of all Mankind," is the true sequence of events as took place on that Thursday night at the Last Supper when her Son prayed for unity and on the following day, Friday, when at the foot of the Cross he bequeathed his mother to be the Mother of all Mankind, of all Peoples, of all Nations. The next time she would identify herself in such a way would be in Amsterdam. The year would be 1945.

> *"Of those who love me, of those who cry to me, of those who have confidence in me. Here I will hear their weeping and their sorrows and will remedy and alleviate their sufferings, necessities and misfortunes."*

D. Roberto, the hermit, wrote in his book *The Love of Mary:* "She loves all in general; but those, who with a special desire to serve her with a tender affection and with fidelity, consecrate themselves to her love and place their whole confidence in her — these indeed are the most precious jewels in her crown, her dearest, her choicest favourites. She not only loves them, but she cherishes them with the partiality and the tenderness of a mother and a spouse, and prefers them to everyone else in graces, favours, love and protection." He goes on to add: "The love that Mary has for us is greater than that of all the mothers and wives in the world. With what emotions, then, of tenderest mercy will she not regard and pity our miseries and hasten to our assistance?"

The great French saint, St. Bernard of Clairvaux (1112–1153), in one of his sermons (*Serm supe Salve Regina*), said: "And she dearly loves them that love her, and she is near to them that call upon her, especially those whom she sees like her in chastity and humility and who, after her divine Son, have placed their hope in her."

On Tuesday, December 12, 1531, when Juan Diego was concerned about his uncle's health, she said to him:

> *"Listen and be sure, my dear son, that I will protect you; do not be frightened or grieved, or let your heart be troubled. Am I not here I who am your mother, and is my help not a refuge? What more do you need? Are you not in the folds of my mantle? Am I not of your kind?"*

But are not these consolations her perfect acknowledgement of and response to the 11th century popular Marian prayers, the *Salve Regina*, and the 13th century *Sub Tuum* (see chapter 16).

A contemporary view of the religious significance of Guadalupe is typified by Virgil Elizondo (1986) when he wrote: "In her, the people experience acceptance, dignity, love and protection. Were it not for Our Lady of Guadalupe there would be no Mexicans or Mexican American people today. The great Mexican nations had been defeated by the Spanish invasion, which came to a violent and bloody climax in 1521. The native peoples who had not been killed no longer wanted to live. Everything of value to them, including their gods, had been destroyed. Nothing was worth living for. With this colossal catastrophe, the entire past became irrelevant…. In sharp contrast to the total rupture with the past which was initiated by the conquest-evangelization enterprise, Guadalupe provided the necessary *sense of continuity* which is basic to human existence…. Out of their own past and in close continuity with it, something truly sacred was now emerging."

And as Sabra McKenzi said: "Thus she restored to a conquered people a sense of worth and dignity, and laid for them a foundation for a revived religious and *national* identity." Jacques Lafaye, in his book *Quetzalcoatl and Guadalupe: The formation of Mexican National Consciousness, 1531–1813,* sees Guadalupe as the one common element in an otherwise fragmented nation that lacked a natural force of unity. Our Lady of Guadalupe is revered for her motherly protection and love, and the Guadalupe apparitions were an opportune sign that the Virgin Mary had chosen Mexico as her "favoured city" and Mexicans as her chosen ones.

But you will have to go to Mexico to see the tilma and to witness the devotion of many Mexicans to their "spiritual" Mother of Guadalupe, particularly on her great feast day on December 12, to understand what this means to "her chosen ones." You will have had to be in Mexico City during the visit of Pope John Paul II in January, 1999 to appreciate the devotion of most of the descendants of the Aztecs to Mary and her *Totus Tuus* Pope. "Viva la Virgen de Guadalupe," and "Juan Pablo Secundo. Te quiere el mundo," were the incessant cries. This, however, is not to say that all Mexicans today are Juan Diegos!

But devotion to *Our Lady of Guadalupe* was not restricted to the Americas. It also spread to Europe in 1571.

Chapter 1 Photos

Ida Peerdeman

Bishop Paolo Hnilica

Bishop Hendrich Bomers

Bishop Josef Punt

Cardinal M. Stickler

Dr. Mark Miravalle

Fr. Paul Sigl

Dr. Mark Miravalle, Fr. Peter Klos and the author

The 3ʳᵈ International Day of Prayer, Amsterdam, 1999

The Sisters of the Family of Mary Co-Redemptrix

Chapter 2 Photos

Edwin Hubble

Albert Einstein

The Milkyway is Milky

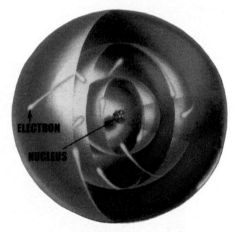

An Atom

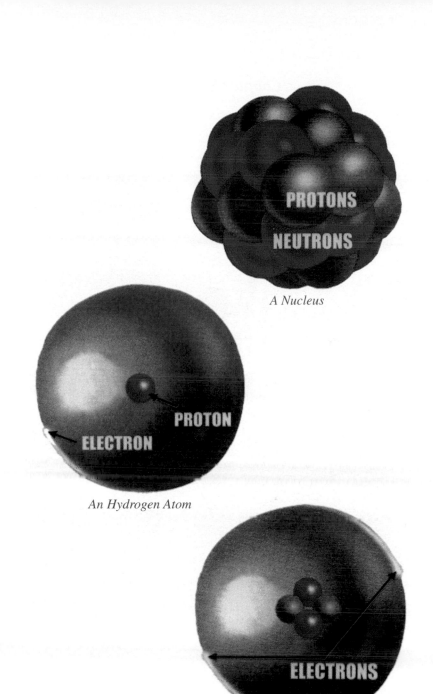

A Nucleus

An Hydrogen Atom

An Helium Atom

A Gustave Doré Illustration of Deborah (Judges 5:1-31)

Jael and the Slain Sisera (Judges 4:21)

Judith with the Head of Holofernes (Judith 13:8)

David Decapitates Goliath (1 Samuel 17:49:51)

Chapter 7 Photos

Hail, Full of Grace

Blessed is the Fruit of Your Womb

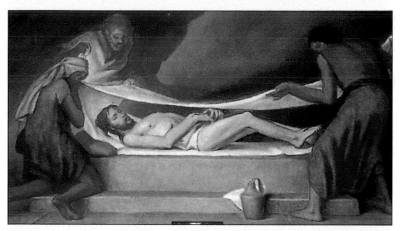

How the Shroud was Wrapped

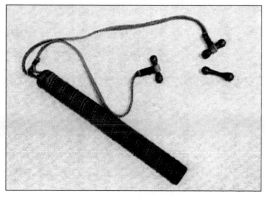

A Roman Flagrum

The Photographic "Negative"

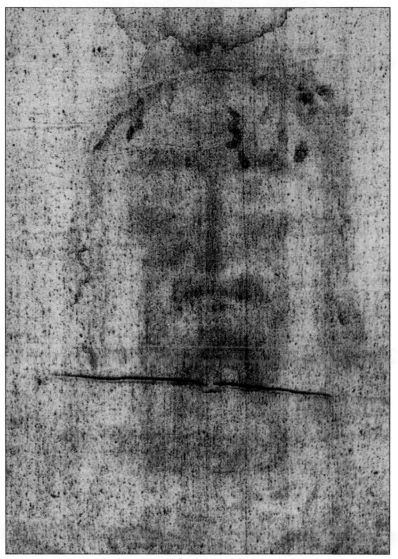

The Photographic "Positive"

The Cap of Thorns

Prof. Max Frei at the Microscope

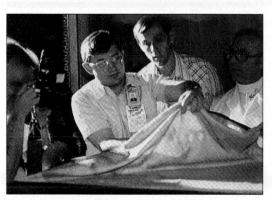

Eric Jumper Examines the
Underside of the Shroud

*A Painting Depicting the Discovery
of the Statue of Our Lady of Guadalupe*

Our Lady of Guadalupe of Extremadura, Spain

Pope John Paul II Visits the Shrine

The Monastery and Shrine of Guadalupe, Spain

Chapter 16 Photos

Christopher Colombus

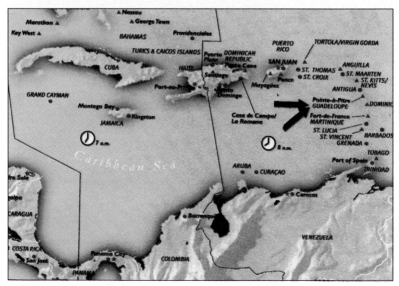

Columbus Discovers the Caribbean

"From the Womb" - Our Lady of Guadalupe
The Immaculate Conception

"To the Tomb" - The Lady of All Nations
The Co-Redemptrix

Chapter 19 Photos

San Stefano d'Aveto in the Mountains

The Replica of the Tilma Behind the Altar

Stained Glass Window of Admiral Andrea Doria

Statue of Our Lady of Guadalupe of Mexico on the Church Lawn

Juan Diego and the Roses from the Garden of Roses

Our Lady of La Salette

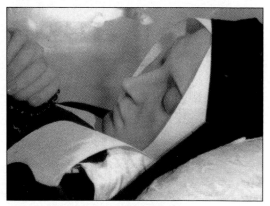

The Incorrupt Body of Bernadette

The Lady of Lourdes with Her Rosary

The Lady of the
Rosary of Fatima

The Lady of Mt. Carmel of Garabandal

Dining at Conchita's Home with Dr. and Mrs. S. Dominguez

Christiane ROMAN-BOCABEILLE

LE MYSTÈRE
DES APPARITIONS
DE GARABANDAL

✝

Queridos Sr. Bartholomew

*con cariño le deseo
que la Santísima Virgen
sea Su Luz para llevarle a
la Felicidad eterna, y en el camino
lleve muchas almas junto a ella*

Pida por mí

Conchita

Conchita's Note

*A Painting Depicting the
Miraculous Host in the Fireplace*

*The Celebration of the Eucharist in the
"Chapel of the Miracle"*

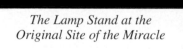

The Lamp Stand at the
Original Site of the Miracle

A Close-up of the Lamp

The Rivers of Amsterdam

The Begijnhof

Tulips in Amsterdam

The Statue of Our Lady of Akita Crying

The Amsterdam–Akita Link

The Statue of Our Lady of All Nations

Chapter 25 Photos

Jerusalem Within the Walls

Jews at the Wailing Wall

Muslims at Prayer

The Jordan River

A Christian Procession in Jerusalem

Chapter 28 Photos

Our Lady of the Eucharist

The Bleeding Host in Betania, Venezuela

The Dream of Don Bosco

The Tombstone of Ida Peerdeman

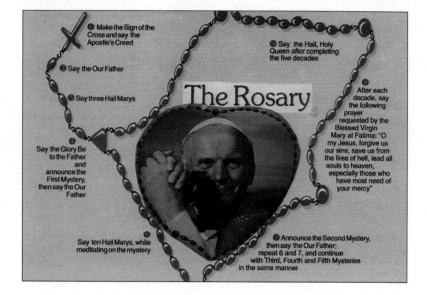

The Rosary

① Make the Sign of the Cross and say the Apostle's Creed

② Say the Our Father

③ Say three Hail Marys

④ Say the Glory Be to the Father and announce the First Mystery, then say the Our Father

⑤ Say ten Hail Marys, while meditating on the mystery

⑥ Announce the Second Mystery, then say the Our Father; repeat 6 and 7, and continue with Third, Fourth and Fifth Mysteries in the same manner

⑦ After each decade, say the following prayer requested by the Blessed Virgin Mary at Fatima: "O my Jesus, forgive us our sins, save us from the fires of hell, lead all souls to heaven, especially those who have most need of your mercy"

⑧ Say the Hail, Holy Queen after completing the five decades

Chapter 19

Our Lady of Guadalupe and the Battle of Lepanto

After more than seven hundred years of struggle, Spain had finally driven out its Muslim rulers, and in 1453 had again become an independent kingdom. In the east, however, there was a resurgence of Islamic power, and a thirst for conquest in the rapidly expanding Turkish (Ottoman) Empire had taken place. The capture of Constantinople by the Turks in 1453 had encouraged their desire to conquer and enslave all of Christendom. Their army invaded the Balkan Peninsula and subjugated all of the eastern Mediterranean countries. By the middle of the 16th century their navy had captured Cyprus and was menacing Venice.

The Turkish plan was to build the greatest navy the world had seen to that time, and then use it to conquer all the European countries bordering on the Mediterranean Sea. From there they would push upward until they had all Europe in their power. Faced with this monstrous threat, Pope Pius V (1566–1572) realized that he had to take drastic action. By skillful diplomacy he persuaded the Spanish and Italian powers to set aside their own rivalries and unite with the Papal squadron to form the Holy League to oppose the advance of the Muslims.

While all this was taking place, Don Fray Alonso de Montufar, the second Archbishop of Mexico, like Bishop Zumurraga, was an enthusiastic champion of Our Lady of Guadalupe. Being very alert to the impending crisis in Europe, he had a small reproduction of the sacred image on Juan Diego's tilma made and touched to the original. He then sent it as a present to King Philip of Spain in 1570. It is said that Archbishop Montufar expressed the hope that when the battle was imminent, the king would place the copy of the sacred image in a suitable location in the Christian navy. King Philip complied and had it mounted in the cabin of Admiral Giovanni Andrea Doria in anticipation of the battle of Lepanto near Greece.

The naval forces of the Holy League assembled. There were two large squadrons, one from Spain, the other from Venice. The smaller squadrons from the Papal States were joined to the Genoese (Italian) forces under Admiral Doria. The supreme command however was given to Don Juan of Austria, half-brother of King Philip of Spain. However, the Christian forces were greatly outnumbered by the Turkish fleet. Their ships were lined up just inside the entrance to the Gulf of Lepanto (now the Gulf of Corinth in Greece), and stretched almost from shore to shore in the form of a crescent. Ali Pasha, the supreme commander of the Turkish fleet, was in the centre.

The allies had formed into three squadrons; in the centre the Spanish ships, to the left the Venetians, and to the right the squadron commanded by Andrea Doria. From the human point of view, the outcome was inevitable, and so, Pope Pius V called upon every Catholic in Europe to invoke the aid of the Mother of God under the title of *Help of Christians,* and to storm heaven unceasingly with Rosaries. The faithful duly responded and the battle got underway.

At a critical moment when it seemed that the Christian forces would lose, a tremendous wind arose and blew the Turkish navy into total disarray. It would be many days afterwards before word reached Rome of the outcome of the battle. But the Pope was mysteriously informed of the result because at the very moment when the victory was gained, he suddenly interrupted a conversation and exclaimed: "Let us give thanks to God. The victory is ours." The Turks lost 230 galleys; the Christians 16. Some 1,500 Christians who had been chained to the oars in the Turkish galleys were freed. It was the last sea battle fought with oar-propelled vessels. The victory of Lepanto brought to an end the Muslim sea-power, never more to be a threat to the Christian world.

The Pope's words were taken down and sealed, and a fortnight later a messenger arrived in Rome announcing the glad tidings of the victory, which took place exactly at the moment when the Pope announced the outcome of the battle on October 7, 1571. The Pope then proclaimed that day a feast day in honour of *Our Lady of Victories*. The following year it was renamed the feast of *Our Lady of the Rosary*. But *Our Lady of Guadalupe's* image was in the cabin of Admiral Doria; she who performed the miracle of the " garden of roses" in Guadalupe, Mexico, 40 years previously in 1531. The word Rosary is from the Latin "rosarium," meaning "a garden of roses."

Admiral Doria lived in San Stefano d'Aveto after the battle (Aveto was the name of a river). The small size reproduction of the sacred image on canvas (about half the size of the original) remained in the possession of the Doria family until 1811, when a descendant, Cardinal Doria, made a present of it to the people of the town of Aveto, north of Genoa, and it has remained there to this very day, enshrined in the Church of San Stefano d'Aveto.

On March 20, 1999, I visited the village church in San Stefano d'Aveto high up in the mountains where a spring originates and where since 1811 the area has been dedicated to Our Lady of Guadalupe. Historians claim that the wood used to make the Italian galleys for the Battle of Lepanto came from that mountainside. The extraordinarily beautiful church houses the replica of the tilma of Juan Diego behind the altar (it was recently restored in Rome in 1989) and outside on the lawn to the right side of the entrance to the church there is a large statue of *Our Lady of Guadalupe* of Mexico on a pedestal with the words inscribed at the base of the statue: "He has done this for no other nation."

The stained glass window in the front of the church depicts an image of Admiral Andrea Doria. I spent over two hours speaking with Fr. Pietro, the parish priest, and three of his Italian friends of the village and was able to appreciate the deep devotion that this area of Italy has for *Our Lady of Guadalupe* of Mexico. There on the mountain top an annual pilgrimage to the statue and to the church is made on August 27. The villagers truly believe that she protected them during World War II. This *Lady of Guadalupe* is also the Immaculate Conception.

Chapter 20

The Third Marian Dogma – The Immaculate Conception

Let us put it this way. Just as we inherit through genetic transference the bodily and other characteristics of our parents, in like manner, at the spiritual level, our souls have inherited the original sin of our first parents. It is the Church's teaching that the stain of this original sin is removed through baptism, which brings sanctifying grace to the soul, thus making it spiritually alive again, *capable* of entering heaven and also making the recipient a member of the Church.

Now, it is true that Paul in Romans 3:23 states that "all have sinned," however, if this is taken with absolute literalness we would then also have to include the man Jesus Christ, which is absurd. Jesus was by nature sinless and did not need redemption. The Immaculate Conception, however, does not refer to the conception of Jesus but means that Mary, whose own conception was brought about the normal way, was nonetheless conceived in the womb of her mother without the stain of original sin. So the Catholic Church dogmatizes.

However, this is not to deny the fact that Mary, too, required a Saviour, for like the other descendants of Adam, by her nature she was subject to the necessity of contracting original sin. But by a special privilege of God, she was preserved from the stain of original sin and certain of its consequences. She was redeemed therefore by the grace of Christ, but in a special way, by anticipation.

And so, just as physical health can come either by way of prevention of disease or by way of curing the disease, so can salvation of the soul. In other words, hers was a "preventive" redemption rather than "curative." She was thus saved or redeemed from the moment of her conception *before* the redemptive act of Jesus by the *anticipatory* expectation and application of that redemptive act on Calvary. It is what led Wordsworth to proclaim that Mary was "our tainted nature's solitary boast."

In receiving this very special kind of baptism at her conception, Mary was the only exception to the universal law. In the scientific sense, one may say that, as in the case of a vaccine, she was immunized against original sin. The Church also believes that by the grace of God Mary, like her son, remained free of every personal sin her whole life long.

Is this teaching scriptural? In fact, there is also no direct statement in the Scriptures which says that the God-man was conceived immaculate, and although there are no direct references to the doctrine of Mary's immaculate conception, there is certainly nothing in Scripture which denies it. There are however a number of indirect scriptural references to support it.

As Mary was uniquely predestined to be the bride of the Holy Spirit (Luke 1:35), to most theologians she obviously had to have a sinless body to bear the God Incarnate, Jesus. Consider also the fall of our first parents. God said to the serpent in the Garden of Eden after the "fall": "I will put enmity between you and the woman, and between your seed and her seed. She will crush your head" (Genesis 3:15). It is therefore through the offspring that she would crush the head of the serpent. This could not be a reference to the first Eve and her offspring Cain. Christian tradition refers to the woman's offspring as Christ for who else but Christ, by the redemptive act of his sacrifice on Calvary, would crush the head of the serpent? If therefore the offspring of the woman is Christ, the "woman" must be Mary, referred to as the second Eve.

However, the prophesized victory of "crushing" the head and power of Satan would not have been a meaningful victory if the conquering Redeemer had assumed his body from a woman who had once been subject to his adversary. His would only have been a pyrrhic victory if his suffering and subsequently glorified body, the very instrument of the victorious redemption (1Cor. 11:24), had been conceived from a mother who had been contaminated or "conquered" by his enemy through sin, even for a moment, for in God's concept one moment in time is very meaningful.

And so, as the Franciscan St. Bonaventure once said: "It was becoming that the Blessed Virgin Mary by whom the devil was to be conquered should never, *even for a moment,* have been under his dominion." In other words, the perfect bride is not one who had given herself to another man — *even for a moment.* As St. Augustine also said as early as the fourth century: "The honour of Christ forbids the least hesitation on this subject of possible sin by his mother," also inferring that she remained sinless throughout her life.

The primary theological reason for Mary's Immaculate Conception given in the encyclical *Ineffabilis Deus* by Pope Pius IX states that she was predestined to be the Theotokos (God-bearer) by the Persons of the Trinity. Other scriptural texts which have been used to support the dogma are found in Luke 1:42: "… and she (Elizabeth) exclaimed with a loud cry: 'Blessed are you among women, and blessed is the fruit of your womb,' and he (Gabriel) came to her and said, 'Hail, full of grace, the Lord is with you.'"

Every law has its exception and it is a maxim that the exception proves and confirms the law. Of this exemption of Mary from the law of spiritual death, the Old Testament Queen Esther is a most interesting illustration. Esther is described in Scripture as being exceedingly fair and of incredible beauty. King Ahasuerus of Persia loved her more than all the women and made her his queen, as related in chapter 7. When she approached the king unannounced, contrary to the law, and revealed her Jewishness to him, he said to her: "What is the matter Esther? Fear not. You shall not die. *This law is not made for you, but for all others.*" And she who was exempted from the law, became the instrument through which her *nation* was saved. She was a prefigure of Mary.

Indeed, Mary is the most wonderful exemption from the common law in so many other ways. No creature ever was before or will be again the *Mother of God.* She is the mother without man's cooperation. She is the Mother of God and man at the same time. She is a mother while remaining a virgin. Her child is born whilst her virginal integrity is preserved. She nourishes God at her breasts. She commands him by her words and he is subject to her. In all these instances, and so many others, she is the exemption to the law.

God made the most perfect of women that could be made when he made the Blessed Virgin for his mother, therefore, he made her sinless and immaculate. That is what St. Bonaventure meant when he wrote: "Mary is that being which God cannot make greater. He can make a greater earth and a greater heaven but not a greater mother." She is the Immaculate Conception, the immaculate preservation, the immunity, the exemption from original sin, all phrases which bear the same significance. But wasn't the first Eve immaculate at birth? Sin had not entered the world as yet. The second Eve was therefore born with the same favourable handicap.

In the 14th and 15th centuries, the great universities and almost all the great religious orders had become bulwarks for the defence of the Immaculate Conception. In the year 1497, the university of Paris unanimously published a statute to the effect that hence forward no one should be admitted as a member of the university who did not swear that he would, to the utmost, assert and defend the position that the Blessed Virgin was preserved and exempted from original sin. Toulouse in France followed the example, and in Italy (Bologna and Naples), in Germany (Cologne, Mayance and Vienna), in Belgium (Louvin), in England before the Reformation (Oxford and Cambridge), in Spain (Salamanca, Toledo, Seville and Valentia), in Portugal (Coimbra and Evora), and in South America (Mexico and Lima), all their great universities and seats of theological learning bound their members by oath to defend the Immaculate Conception.

But it was the Franciscan theologian John Duns Scotus (1266–1308) who was chiefly responsible for introducing the notion of "preservative" redemption into the explicit consciousness of the Church, which was a major breakthrough in helping pave the way for its dogmatic definition. Defenders of the privilege also produced an enormous literature on the subject and between 1600 and 1800 the Jesuits alone brought out three hundred works on the Immaculate Conception. Ruling princes supported the doctrine, and the royal house of Spain sent several delegations to Rome to request the definition of it.

Indeed, in 1648, King Juan of Portugal consecrated and dedicated his country to Mary under the title of the Immaculate Conception, and since then no king or queen of Portugal ever wore a crown. It was reserved for the Immaculate Conception! In 1781, the first church built in my home town, Port of Spain, Trinidad, was also dedicated to the Blessed Virgin under the name of the Immaculate Conception, now a Cathedral.

But Marian theology and devotion deteriorated during the age of the Enlightenment and the revolution which followed it. The revival came from an unexpected source — the apparition of the "Miraculous Medal" in the Rue du Bac, Paris, in 1830. The final stage of development of the dogma of the Immaculate Conception was thus effected to the accompaniment of a spreading movement of the prayer: "O Mary conceived without sin, pray for us who have recourse to thee."

Pope Pius IX took note of the increasing demand during the pontificate of his immediate predecessor Gregory XVI, and the early years of his own, for a dogmatic definition of the Marian privilege. It had come from bishops, the secular clergy, religious orders, sovereign rulers and the faithful. That he might proceed with great prudence, he established a special congregation of cardinals and also selected priests, both secular and regular, well-trained in the theological sciences, bidding them to consider the matter and report to him.

Of twenty theologians whom the Pope consulted in 1848, seventeen gave a favourable reply. To a preliminary meeting of the Congregation of Cardinals, he put two questions: "Should he define the privilege? How?" To the first, they answered affirmatively, and to the second they advised consultation of the bishops. A letter *Ubi Primum* was sent from Gaeta, dated February 2, 1849. It asked the bishops to inform the Pope about the devotion of the faithful as well as the clergy regarding the Immaculate Conception, and the desire for a papal definition. Of 603 bishops consulted, 546 favoured the definition, 4 opposed and the remainder were undecided either as to its opportuness or timing.

And so, on December 8, in that memorable year 1854, during the celebration of a solemn Mass by Pope Pius IX, surrounded by 152 bishops, 53 cardinals, more than 200 prelates, a vast body of clergy from many countries, and some 30 or 40 thousand people who crowded the vast Basilica of St. Peter's, Cardinal Machhi, the Dean of the Sacred College, advanced to the Pontifical throne, accompanied by an archbishop of the Greek Rite, an archbishop of the Armenian Rite and by 12 of the senior archbishops of the western Church, as supporters, and addressed the Pope with these words: "For a long time, most blessed Father, has the Catholic Church most ardently wished and entreated with all her desires, that, in your supreme and infallible judgement, you define the Immaculate Conception of the most Holy Virgin Mary, Mother of God, for the increase of her praise, glory and veneration. In the name of the Sacred College of Cardinals, bishops of the Catholic world, and of all the faithful, we humbly and earnestly entreat of you that on this solemnity of the conception of the Most Blessed Virgin, our common vows may be fulfilled...."

To these words the Pontiff answered: "We declare, pronounce, and define that the doctrine which holds that the Most Blessed Virgin Mary, in the first instant of her conception, by a singular grace and privilege granted by Almighty God, in view of the merits of Jesus Christ, the Saviour, was preserved from all stain of original sin, and is a doctrine revealed by God and therefore to be believed firmly and constantly by all the faithful."

But she had to be the Immaculate Conception in order to house in her womb the true Bread of Life, who gives himself to us daily in the Eucharistic miracle.

Chapter 21

The Rosary – From Guadalupe to Garabandal

It was a garden of roses which was the miracle she performed on Tepeyac hill in Guadalupe, Mexico, in 1531, and which was given so that the bishop would believe in her apparitions. It was in my opinion her first hint of identifying herself with the Rosary. I say this because the name "Rosary" is derived from the Latin "rosarium," meaning "a rose garden."

Now, the rose is indisputably the most beautiful of all the flowers. It is the queen of the flowers. It is a lover's token: "My love is like a red, red rose." Mystical Rose is one of her titles in the Litany of Loreto for she is the most beautiful flower in Paradise. Tightly closed in the bud, it reveals itself in gradual bloom, its petals glistening with the morning dewdrops like tears gently falling to the ground. If its colour is golden yellow it reflects the precious and regal Ark of the Covenant that she is. If its colour is white it can be compared to the "lily of the valley," that pure and immaculate Virgin. If its colour is red it is the colour of the blood of her Son spilled on the Cross for our redemption. And so, there is no rose without a thorn!

The Rosary as a meditative prayer is a firm and constant tradition within the Catholic Church, supported by thirteen Pontiffs since, as tradition has it, Mary first revealed the Rosary devotion to St. Dominic in the early 1200s. To pray the Rosary is simply to contemplate with Mary the Lord made flesh, crucified, and raised for our salvation. In 1569, the Dominican Pope Pius V officially approved the Rosary, which had been completed by the addition of the second half of the *Hail Mary* and the *Glory be to the Father.*

Fundamentalists criticize the Rosary, saying, among other things, that in the Rosary ten prayers are said to Mary for every one said to the Father. Of course, that only displays a total lack of understanding and significance of this most beautiful prayer. In fact the Rosary is a very Christ-centered prayer and thirteen of the fifteen Rosary mysteries are explicitly dedicated to the life of Jesus. The first part of the *Hail Mary* is a joining together of the two greetings in Scripture, one to Mary by the angel Gabriel: "Hail, full of grace, the Lord is with you" (Luke 1:28) and the other to Mary by her cousin Elizabeth: "Blessed are you among women, and blessed is the fruit your womb" (Luke 1:42). It was after these words of greeting that Christianity began. These were the words that are to this day, even in heaven where she is, especially dear to her. It is the privilege for which she is ever grateful in eternity as she was in time.

But the words of the *Hail Mary*, repetitive as they are, are simply background music, as it were, to the recitation of the joyful, sorrowful and glorious mysteries as we contemplate the lives of Jesus and his mother. In the second half of the prayer, we say: "Hail Mary, Mother of God, pray for us sinners now and at the hour of our death. Amen." Surely, if Christ could have his mother praying at the foot of the Cross at the hour of his death, should we not also want to have her at our death bed, praying for us and with us at the hour of our death?

La Salette

Following the miracle of the garden of roses on Tepeyac hill in Guadalupe, Mexico, in 1531, three centuries later in 1846, she appeared in the Alpine village of La Salette. She was crying as a mother in great distress over a peril threatening her children. As Melanie Calvat, one of the two visionaries, testified: "The Holy Virgin was crying nearly the whole time that she was speaking to me. Her tears flowed gently, one by one, down to her knees, then like sparks of light they disappeared. These tears of our sweet mother, far from lessening her air of majesty, of a queen, seemed on the contrary to embellish her, to make her more beautiful, more powerful, more filled with love, more maternal, more ravishing. Is it possible to see a mother cry, and such a mother, without doing anything possible to comfort her and change her grief into joy?"

She continued: "The clothing of the most Holy Virgin was silver-white and quite brilliant, and the *crown of roses* which she wore upon her head was so beautiful that it defied imagination. It formed a most beautiful diadem which shone brighter than the earth's sun." This colourful crown of roses on her head is depicted in drawings with the colours red, yellow and white. In short, "a garden of roses" was upon her head like a crown of stars. It was another symbol of her favourite prayer, the Rosary.

She prophesied future calamities for Europe and the world and lamented the lack of observation of Sunday as the day of the Lord, and also the frequent swearing, using the name of her Son.

Lourdes

But it was in Lourdes in 1858 that she actually carried a Rosary for the first time. Bernadette suddenly saw a golden-coloured cloud which preceded a light. It was a light "more brilliant than the sun." In the midst of this supernatural light a young Lady appeared in an instant. Shades of Guadalupe and La Salette! She seemed to come out of the depth of a niche cut into the rock. She was dressed in a white garment that also shone brilliantly, with a long white veil which, covering her head, came down over her shoulders. Her garment was gathered at the waist by a blue cincture fastened with one bow. Her feet, resting on a carpet of grass and twigs, were bare, but upon each one there was a golden rose.

J.B. Estrade, a government official, had faithfully recorded the actual testimony of Bernadette during her investigation by the French authorities in 1858: "Without thinking what I was doing, I took my Rosary in my hands and went on my knees. The Lady made a sign of approval with her head and took into her hands a Rosary which hung on her right arm. When I attempted to begin the Rosary and tried to lift my hand to my forehead, my arm remained paralyzed, and it was only after the Lady had signed herself that I could do the same. The Lady left me to pray alone. She passed the beads of her Rosary between her fingers but said nothing. Only at the end of each decade did she say the *'Gloria'* with me."

This last detail reveals a deep theological truth. The *Gloria,* which is a hymn of praise to the Trinity, is indeed the only part of the Rosary which is suitable to the Virgin. The *Our Father* is certainly not for one who had no need to pray for her daily bread. As for the *Hail Mary,* the angel's greeting, this could only be recited by Bernadette, as the apparition had no need to greet her own self.

On March 25, 1858, the sixteenth apparition, Bernadette asked the Lady her name. She had previously done so on three occasions, but this time the Virgin, who until then had kept her hands joined together that day, opened her arms and lowered them, thus causing her Rosary to slip down towards her wrist. Then she joined her hands again, brought them above her breasts, raised her eyes to heaven in an expression of reverential gratitude and humility, and said: "I am the Immaculate Conception."

Fatima

But it was in Fatima that she actually spoke the words which she had hinted in Guadalupe with the garden of roses, in La Salette (the crown of roses), and in Lourdes (the Rosary beads). On October 13, 1917, she said to the young visionaries: "I am the Lady of the Rosary."

On Sunday, May 13, 1917, while World War I was raging, the Blessed Virgin Mary appeared to three children – Lucia, Jacinta and Francisco. It was just after noon. The children saw something "like a small cloud" come down upon a little holm oak tree in the Cova da Iria. To quote Lucia's own words: "We beheld a Lady all dressed in white. She was more brilliant than the sun and radiated a light more clear and intense than a crystal glass filled with sparkling water, the rays of the burning sun shining through it." This, of course, is how she also appeared in Guadalupe, La Salette and Lourdes.

She said to the children: "I come from heaven.... I want you to come here on the thirteenth of each month until October when I will tell you who I am and what I want." Then rising from the top of the little holm oak tree, she glided away into the sky towards the east. As she departed the upper leaves of the little oak tree remained for several hours stretched and bending towards the east.

She wore a white mantle falling to her feet edged in burnished gold. A prominent star shone from the hem of her robe. It was her calling card. It was the symbol that she came to Fatima as the second Esther. In the Old Testament Queen Esther saved her Jewish people from annihilation on the thirteenth day of the month of Adar. The word Esther means "star." But from her hand hung an exquisite Rosary of white pearls. It was her spiritual weapon to prevent wars and annihilation. She said: "Say the Rosary to obtain peace for the world and the end of the war."

In her first apparition on May 13 (and on all subsequent apparitions), the Blessed Virgin stood on the branch of a holm oak tree. Recent scientific research on tiny material from the head area of the Shroud of Turin removed by Scotch tape showed microscopic pieces of wood which had the characteristic structure of tubules from oak wood. It has also been tradition that the Cross was made from holm oak. History also records that at the time of Christ the oak was the most common tree in Palestine. And so, the Co-Redemptrix came to Fatima standing on the wood of the Cross!

On September 13, she briefly said: "Continue to say the Rosary to bring about the end of the war." It was brief, concise, and to the point. It emphasized succinctly the power of the Rosary. But it was on October 13 that the great miracle of the sun took place. The sun moved from its abode in the sky and came plunging down to earth, but at the command of Her Majesty, the Queen of heaven and earth, the sun was seen to retreat to its celestial abode. But what also made that miracle unique is that its exact time and location, albeit, not its nature, was publicly announced months in advance by the visionaries. The miracle was even reported by the leading anti-clerical newspapers in Portugal at the time — *Diario de Noticias (Daily News)* and another Government newspaper *O Seculo (The Century)*.

The miracle was seen over a 600-square-mile area, thus obviating the suggested explanation of collective hallucination. An Italian Jesuit scientist, Tio Sciapizzi, a professor of algebra and trigonometry at the Gregorian University in Rome, and an outstanding mathematician and astronomer, undertook an exhaustive study of the phenomenon and concluded: "Of the historic reality of this event there can be no doubt whatsoever. That it was outside and against known laws can be proved by certain simple scientific considerations.... Given the indubitable reference to God and the general context of the event, it seems that we must attribute to him alone the most obvious and colossal miracle of history."

Now, in 1917 scientists knew relatively little about the chemical composition of the sun compared to what we know now. Close to a million miles in diameter, it is a gaseous body composed mainly of hydrogen. But it was only in the early 1930s (after the Fatima apparitions) that Atkinson and Houtermans showed that nuclear transformation processes occur in the solar interior. Every second that passes, the sun compresses 564 million tons of hydrogen into 560 million tons of helium, the second lightest element and 4 million tons of matter are then released as energy. Like all the stars, the sun generates its energy by a nuclear process known as nuclear fusion. It is this nuclear reaction which illuminates the sky, gives warmth to the atmosphere, and sustains life on earth. It is the fusion of two molecules of hydrogen into helium.

This indeed is the principle behind the making of the hydrogen bomb. In short, the sun is nothing but a huge hydrogen bomb which has been continuously exploding for the past 5 billion years! The miracle of the sun should now be looked upon differently. I believe that it is symbolic of the possible annihilation of nations as the Virgin Mary warned on June 13.

In his book *Crossing The Threshold Of Hope,* Pope John Paul II says on page 221: "And thus we come to May 13, 1981, when I was wounded by gunshots fired in St. Peter's Square. At first I did not pay attention to the fact that the assassination attempt had occurred on the exact anniversary of the day Mary appeared to the three children at Fatima in Portugal and spoke to them the words that now, at the end of this century, seem to be close to their fulfillment." But it was on October 13 in Fatima that she identified herself to the visionaries: "I am the Lady of the Rosary." It was her answer to the threat of the nuclear annihilation of nations.

But on the very day the Blessed Virgin Mary first came to the children in the Cova da Iria, a young Vatican diplomat named Eugenio Pacelli (one day to be Pope Pius XII) was consecrated archbishop in the Sistine Chapel. He was to be the Pope who would proclaim the fourth Marian Dogma, the Assumption of the Blessed Virgin Mary.

Garabandal

During the miracle of the sun on October 13, 1917, the children of Fatima also saw the Blessed Virgin in the garb of Our Lady of Mount Carmel with a Scapular hanging on her right hand. When Lucia was asked why Our Lady appeared in the sky in her very last apparition holding the Scapular in her hand, she said that it is because she wants everyone to wear it. She added: "It is a sign of consecration to the Immaculate Heart of Mary." And on another occasion she said: "It is because the Rosary and the Scapular are one."

Now, San Sebastian of Garabandal is a poor village in the Cantabrian mountains, 35 miles southwest of Santander in Spain. Its 300 inhabitants led an austere and laborious life and raised sheep and cattle. They were very religious and there was a time-honoured custom of meeting everyday in the church to recite the Rosary.

On Sunday June 18, 1961, at 8:30 p.m., four young children of Garabanbal heard a "noise like thunder," then they saw a beautiful angel appear in a gulf of brilliant light. He quickly disappeared. On Saturday July 1, 1961, towards 7:30 p.m., the same angel appeared again to the children and announced to them that on the following Sunday the Blessed Virgin would appear to them under the title of the Lady of Mount Carmel.

So said, around 6:00 p.m., on July 2, at that time the feast of the Visitation, the Blessed Virgin appeared to them at the Pines accompanied by St. Michael and another angel not identified by the visionaries. She appeared in a white garment and a blue mantle with a crown of golden stars on her head. Her hands were delicate but her feet were not visible. The Scapular which she wore on her right wrist was of a brownish colour with a small mountain designed on it. Her hair was of a deep chestnut colour, long, slightly waved and parted in the middle. Her complexion was tan and her voice was very sweet and musical. She asked them to say the Rosary daily and taught them to recite it slowly and with reverence. On the following day, July 3, she appeared with the Child Jesus on her left arm.

Now, some people in the fall of 1961 felt that she could not be Our Lady of Mount Carmel because of her garb, but she appeared once to Conchita afterwards dressed as a Carmelite nun in a traditional brown dress, saying: "I am one and the same."

The apparitions took place from July 2, 1961 to January 20, 1963, the feast day of St. Sebastian, patron saint of the parish. On October 18, 1961, Michael delivered this message to the little children on behalf of the Virgin. (It is said that she did not have the courage, as it were, to tell it to the children herself. Such is her motherly tenderness and sensitivity!): "Before the cup was filling up, now it is overflowing. Many cardinals, bishops, and many priests are on the road to perdition and are taking many souls with them. Less and less importance has been given to the Eucharist.... I, your mother, through the intercession of St. Michael the Archangel, ask you to mend your lives. You are now receiving the last warnings. I love you very much and do not wish your condemnation. Pray to us in sincerity and we will grant your requests. You should make more sacrifices. Think of the Passion of Jesus."

In her last apparition to the children on November 13, 1965, the Virgin's closing remarks to Conchita, one of the young visionaries, were: "Conchita, why do you not go more often to visit my Son in the Tabernacle. He waits for you there day and night." She also said: "Remember that I told you that when you present yourself before God your hands must be filled with good works done for your brothers and for the glory of God. But at the present time your hands are empty."

It was only after reading this that I came to understand more clearly why Conchita inscribed certain words (in Spanish) to me on the front page of a book on Garabanbal, which she gave to me as a gift when I was a dinner guest at her home on August 29, 1989. Translated in english, it reads: "With love it is my wish that the Blessed Virgin would be your light to lead you to eternal happiness, and that on the way you will bring many souls to her. Pray for me, Conchita."

And so, the ultimate message of Garabandal is adoration of the Eucharist and recitation of the Rosary. So it also was in Fatima. The Angel of Peace, the guardian angel of Portugal, believed to be St. Michael, had appeared to the visionaries in the spring of 1916 before the appearance of Her Majesty. He taught them to adore Jesus in the Eucharist.

Chapter 22

Amsterdam – The City of the Eucharistic Miracle, 1345 AD

Because the Blessed Virgin chose Amsterdam to appear to Ida Peerdeman in 1945, I decided to research the history of Amsterdam. It is recorded that the earliest inhabitants of what is now Holland were three tribes that settled the marshy deltas of the "lowlands" sometime in the dawn of recorded history. There was the ferocious Belgae of the southern regions; the opportunistic Batavi, who settled in the area of the great rivers, and the fiercely independent Frisians who took residence along the northern coasts. In the 8th century, the mighty Charlemagne (Charles the Great), king of the Franks and emperor of the West, managed to force the Frisians to give up their pagan gods in exchange for Christianity.

Founded around the 13th century, Amsterdam stood at the confluence of the Amstel and Ij rivers, and to protect themselves against floods, the early inhabitants built a dyke (dam) across the Amstel River, which gave birth to the name Amstelledamme, then called Amsteldam and later Amsterdam. It is the home of the modern tulip, and its appearance means that spring has truly arrived. The world "tulip" comes from the Turkish word "tulipan," meaning turban, being truly similar in shape to a turban. To Persians it is a symbol of love. In an old Persian myth a young man named Ferhad, suffering from unrequited love, wandered into the desert and it is said that each of his hopeless tears was transformed into a red tulip!

The city has more than twelve hundred bridges spanning its nearly two hundred canals. In fact, Amsterdam is called the Venice of the North by reason of its great number of canals, which are to be found along almost every street. In 1306, work began on the first religious edifice. It was the Catholic Church later to be known as the *Oude Kerk* (Old Church). St. Nicholas was chosen as the city's patron saint and the *Oude Kerk* was originally named after him. About forty years later, the Eucharistic miracle of Amsterdam occurred on March 15, 1345, in a house on Kalverstraat. It was exactly 600 years before the first apparition of the *Mother of all Nations* on March 25, 1945, as there is a time difference of ten days between the present Gregorian calendar and the Julian calendar which was in use at that time.

A man named Ysbrant Dommer, seriously ill and near death, was given Holy Communion after confession by the parish priest. Shortly after the priest left the house, the patient became violently ill and vomited. The woman attendant, having collected the vomitus in a basin, threw it into a large open fire in the hearth. The next morning when she went to the hearth to revive the embers, she was startled to see the Host, fresh and brilliant among the coals, which still supported a low flame. She instinctively snatched the Host from the fire, carefully wrapped it in a clean linen cloth, and placed it in a chest for safe keeping. The priest, who was immediately summoned, placed the Host in a pyx, and carried it to the parish church of St. Nicholas. The following morning, to his surprise, he found the pyx empty, but the Host was discovered by the same woman when she opened the chest in the house to remove some linens.

Once more, the priest was summoned and he decided to return the Host to the church. Then, after yet another disappearance and discovery, flabbergasted, he finally assembled other members of the clergy for consultation. They all agreed that the occurrences were a direct proof of God's intervention, and apparently a sign that the miracle should be publicly honoured. The miraculous Host was then carried in solemn procession to the Church of St. Nicholas, and the following year the bishop officially declared the whole event a miracle. The house in which the miracle took place was soon turned into a chapel called *Helige Stede* or the

Holy Place, and the fireplace in which the miracle first took place was carefully preserved.

About 100 years later, in 1452, when the population was about 5,000, a great fire destroyed most of the mainly-wooden town of Amsterdam and inflamed the Holy Place (interestingly, the fire left the *Oude Kerk* untouched). When the fire was finally extinguished another miracle was discovered. Lying amidst the smoldering ruins, untouched by the fire, was the pyx containing the miraculous Host together with its silken cover. The chapel was then rebuilt and enormous crowds began to flock there and also participated in annual processions on the Saturday night following the anniversary date of the miracle.

In 1486, when Maximilian I of Austria, later to become a Holy Roman Emperor, fell gravely ill in the south of Holland, he swore that if he recovered he would make a pilgrimage to the chapel. Maximilian visited Amsterdam two years later and dedicated a stained glass window to the church and presented embroidered cushions. In 1489, he gave Amsterdam the crown of the Holy Roman Empire, "since it is not adorned with a coat of arms such as it ought to have," he said. Charles V, King of Spain and the Holy Roman Emperor, also came to Amsterdam in 1532, the year after the Virgin appeared in Guadalupe, Mexico, and word of kings walking in the Amsterdam procession drew hordes of the faithful.

During the Middle Ages, Holland was a bastion of Catholicism, with powerful bishoprics in the cities of Utrecht and Maastrich, until 1578, when the Reformation, begun by Martin Luther in 1517, condemned the Catholic religion in Holland to two hundred years of semi-clandestine existence. When the city went over to the Protestant Prince William of Orange's side in 1578, the silent processions were immediately forbidden and the chapel fell into disuse. Indeed, between 1578 and 1815 the Catholics, though tolerated, were forced to exercise the utmost discretion and to worship in secret.

Around that time nations throughout Europe wrestled with the notion of religious diversity. In Spain, this resulted in the infamous Inquisition, which was designed to rid the realm of such "heretics" as Lutherans, Jews, and intellectuals. Among the more radical Protestant sects were the Anabaptists, some of whom had left Germany in 1530 in hope of finding a more tolerant climate in Amsterdam. The Anabaptists rejected the Catholic celebration of saints' days and infant baptism, favouring adult baptism instead. They also did not believe in the Trinity.

Now, as a Catholic and then a Protestant city, Amsterdam has always been a melting pot for many different nationalities and religions. From the 16th century onwards Portuguese and German Jews settled in the east of Amsterdam, the only city in Europe to allow them freedom of worship. Jewish refugees fleeing persecution in other European countries found a tolerant haven, religious freedom and friendly acceptance in the Dutch capital city, and for over four centuries Amsterdam was known as "New Jerusalem" or "Jerusalem of the West." The Jews also called the city *Makum,* from the Hebrew *Makum aleph,* "the best city of all."

Following the Reformation, Calvinist iconoclasm raged in Amsterdam, leading to serious damage being done to Catholic churches. Bands of Calvinists, Lutherans, and Anabaptists scoured the country "thirsting for the blood of papists and the possessions of the rich." They plundered four hundred churches, maltreated the monks, priests and nuns, desecrated the Sacred Species, and committed other acts of sacrilege and violence.

In 1572, nineteen priests and brothers in a little town on the seacoast of Holland eventually became known as the Martyrs of Gorcum. On June 26, an armed force under the Baron de la Marque sailed into Gorcum and took over the town. They were really pirates, but they were also staunch Calvinists whose anti-Spanish politics meshed comfortably with their anti-Catholic theology. They were convinced that Catholicism had to be wiped out, and they began rounding up all the priests and brothers they could find. These clergymen were mocked by being forced to process around the town's square singing the Litany of the Saints. Calvinist ministers were brought in to interrogate the Catholic clergymen so that they could be harangued with the "new discoveries" of Calvinist theology.

The ministers zeroed in on the Catholic belief in the Real Presence of Christ in the Eucharist, and vehemently denied it, declaring that Communion is only a memorial meal, and that it is not necessary to have priests in order to have the Eucharist. However, the Catholic prisoners refused to deny one iota of the Catholic

Church's doctrine on the Blessed Sacrament. At this the pirate-admiral proclaimed that they could all go free if they would publicly disavow the Eucharist and the papacy. The Gorcum priests adamantly refused to do so and stood their grounds courageously.

Just after midnight on July 9, 1572, they were hanged from roof beams, then they were cut down and their bodies dumped into an inglorious grave where they remained unhonoured for over forty years. During a truce between Spain and Holland, permission was eventually granted to exhume the bodies and to bring the sacred remains to Brussels, where they were enshrined in a Franciscan church. Pope Pius IX, the Pope of the dogma of the Immaculate Conception, declared these priests to be saints in 1867.

In 1578, Amsterdam went over to the Protestant party and all of Amsterdam's Catholic churches became Protestant, including the *Oude Kerk* or Old Church. Calvinism then became the official religion in Amsterdam. The Catholics then went underground with their clandestine churches and by 1658 there were twenty-six hidden houses of prayer in Amsterdam. The Host disappeared during the Protestant ascendancy in Amsterdam, but the chapel was still the destination of annual pilgrimages, organized by a Dutch religious group, which took place on the Saturday night following the anniversary date of the miracle on March 15, 1345. On Rocking near the dam still stands a monument commemorating the 1345 miracle.

Now, when the chapel housing the miraculous Host was confiscated by the city authorities at the time of the Reformation, the Host was given into the care of the Beguines in the *Begijnhof*, a community consisting of lay women who took temporary vows of obedience and chastity. Individual processions had taken place throughout the years since the time of the miracle and continued even during the Reformation, when they were called "silent processions" because the people would walk along the Holy Way in silence, as a private devotion.

On Saturday, March 20, 1999, I joined friends in Amsterdam for the silent procession throughout the night. We first went to a solemnly sung High Mass at 10:30 p.m. in the *Begijnhof* chapel and then joined a large group of pilgrims in the hour-long silent procession, which included part of today's red light district. Contrary to what I expected, the procession does not begin at any fixed time. Catholics throughout Amsterdam and bus loads of pilgrims from other parts of the country and neighbouring states arrived at various times processing throughout the night. Not a word was spoken or heard, and men in special orange jackets were strategically placed to direct the marchers to the proper route of the procession. It was an experience that I will hardly forget, a Catholic minority silently manifesting their Eucharistic devotion. It may be said that it was the Dutch equivalent of Corpus Christi processions in certain Catholic countries.

The little chapel house in which the miracle occurred was demolished in 1908 over the protests of both Catholics and Protestants. However, the chapel is far from being forgotten, since its likeness has been captured in a stained glass window in the new chapel of the *Begijnhof*. In commemoration of the miracle, the Blessed Sacrament is daily exposed for adoration in this chapel. Thus Amsterdam has become a place of pilgrimage for the whole of the Netherlands. The Begijnhof chapel is now the starting and finishing point of the silent procession and is also referred to as the "miracle chapel."

Nowadays 25 percent of Amsterdammers are foreign born. The population, which is nearing 750,000, includes 175 different nationalities, with the largest ethnic groups from Suriname, Turkey, Morocco and the Dutch Antilles. But times have changed. Amsterdam is no longer as religious or Catholic as it was in 1345. The "Empire" struck back. In the 1960s, the city became the hippie capital of Europe, and today the square around the Oude Kerk is right next to the official prostitution district. The visitor is therefore forced to switch abruptly from looking at the oldest church in Amsterdam or from hearing a concert of organ music by Bach to a display of prostitutes' windows. The area is also frequented by drug dealers and here too are found the great majority of Amsterdam's marijuana-selling coffee shops.

Yet it is in this *multinational* city, where the Blessed Virgin appeared in 1945, that the movement for the promotion of the veneration of Our Lady as the *Mother of All Nations* and for the propagation of her request for a fifth and final Marian dogma — Mary, Co-Redemptrix, Mediatrix and Advocate — has started.

It was on the Thursday night that the Redeemer instituted the Holy Eucharist. On the following day the first High Mass was celebrated on Calvary. It was the bloody sacrifice of the Lamb. The unbloody sacrifice has been celebrated daily ever since. She chose Amsterdam, this multinational city where a Eucharistic miracle occurred, to appear as the *Lady, Mary, Mother of all Nations,* standing in front of the Cross where she suffered so much during the sacrifice of her Son. It will in time be intimately linked to a little town in Akita, Japan, in a very prophetic and spiritual way.

Chapter 23

The Amsterdam, Akita, Medjugorje Link

In 1945, the Blessed Virgin Mary appeared to Ida Peerdeman in Amsterdam on March 25, the feast of the Annunciation, as the Lady, Mary, Mother of all Nations. It was towards the end of World War II. Twenty eight years after appearing there, a statue of the Virgin in Akita, Japan, wept 101 times between 1973 and 1981. Of significant interest is that the statue, as carved by a famed Japanese sculptor, is a close replica of the painting of the Lady, Mary, Mother of all Nations as she appeared to Ida Peerdeman.

On August 3, 1973, Sr. Agnes Sasagawa, a nun of the Order of the Handmaids of the Eucharist (the Virgin appeared in Fatima in 1917 on the feast of Our Lady of the Eucharist), heard a voice of indescribable beauty coming from a wooden statue in the chapel: "My daughter, my novice, listen to what I have to say to you. It is very important. You will convey it to your Superior. Many people in this world offend the Lord.... In order that the world might know his anger, the heavenly Father is preparing a great chastisement on all mankind. With my Son, I have intervened so many times to appease the wrath of the Father. I have prevented the onset of calamities by offering the sufferings of the Son on the Cross, his precious blood, and the beloved souls who console him and form a cohort of victim souls...."

Then on October 13, the anniversary date of her last apparition in Fatima in 1917 and of the miracle of the sun, Sr. Agnes heard the beautiful voice speaking once more from the statue: "The work of the devil will infiltrate even into the Church in such a way that one would see cardinals opposing cardinals, bishops against other bishops. The priests who venerate me will be scorned and opposed by their confreres. Churches and altars will be sacked. The Church will be full of those who accept compromises and the devil will press many priests and consecrated souls to leave the service of the Lord. The demon will be especially implacable against souls consecrated to God. The thought of the loss of so many souls is the cause of my sadness. If sins increase in number and gravity, there will no longer be any pardon for them."

She continued: "As I told you, if people do not repent and better themselves, the Father will inflict a terrible punishment on all humanity. It will be a punishment greater than the Flood, such as one will never have seen before. Fire will fall from the sky and wipe out a great part of humanity, the good as well as the bad, sparing neither priests nor faithful. The survivors will find themselves so desolate that they will envy the dead. The only arms which will remain for you will be the Rosary and the Sign left by my Son. Each day recite the prayers of the Rosary. With the Rosary pray for the Pope, the bishops, the priests."

The statue wept for the last time on September 15, 1981. It was the feast of Our Lady of Sorrows. But why such an apocalyptic message in Japan? It is obvious that it is because two cities in Japan had already experienced their own apocalypse. I refer to Hiroshima and Nagasaki. In 1945, the atomic bomb was dropped on these two cities and over a million and a half people were annihilated in seconds. The survivors envied the dead!

Now, 28 years after the end of World War I in 1918, the Blessed Virgin Mary appeared in Amsterdam towards the end of World War II in 1945. Then 28 years after the end of World War II, she appeared in 1973, in Akita, Japan, where the atomic bomb fell, and gave her apocalyptic message. If we follow this mathematical progression, 28 years after 1973 will be the year 2001. I am drawing no conclusion. I am simply stating a mathematical fact, which may or may not be of any significance. However, in an attempt to determine the probable significance of the number 28, I resorted to the history of the calendar. In the measurement of time the rotation of the earth on its axis measures the 24 hour day, the revolution of the moon around the earth gives the lunar month ($29\frac{1}{2}$ days), and the revolution of the earth around the sun makes a solar year (365.2422 days). The solar cycle is 28 years! This cycle was designed to show the relation between the day of the week and the day of the month. If there were no leap years, the day of the week and the day of the month would show a regular correspondence in a series lasting seven years because there are seven different weekdays, and the year may begin with any one. And so, could it be that the number 28 was symbolically associated with a cycle of events, in this case, the solar cycle?

Indeed, like many different peoples and cultures that had preceded them in Mexico, the Aztecs, to whom the Blessed Virgin appeared on Tepeyac hill in Mexico in 1531, believed that the universe operated in great cycles. The priests stated as a matter of simple fact that there had been four such cycles or "suns" (in this case, not as short as 28 year intervals) since the creation of the human race. At the time of the Spanish conquest it was the fifth "sun" that prevailed. Indeed, as Graham Hancock said in his book *Fingerprints of the Gods*, "for these people just about everything boiled down to numbers, the passage of the years and the manifestations of events. The belief was that if numbers which lay beneath the manifestations could be properly understood, it would be possible to predict successfully the timing of the events themselves." But numbers also play a significant role in the Bible. Indeed, once while I was in Jerusalem I was discussing this with a Hebrew scholar and she said that "theomatics" is the word they use in relation to the study of such numbers in the old Hebrew Bible.

Eight years after Akita, in 1981, the Blessed Virgin appeared in Medjugorje on the feast of John the Baptist, June 24. John prepared the way for the First Coming of her Son. Is it therefore that she is preparing us for the Second Coming? She has been appearing there every day since then, exhorting the world to prayer, conversion and the recitation of the Rosary. Like in Lourdes, Fatima and Akita, Eucharistic adoration also plays a major role in the devotion of this shrine in Medjugorje.

But why did she choose Yugoslavia to appear as the Queen of Peace, significantly, the very last of her titles in the Litany of

Loreto? It is undoubtedly because the spark that ignited World War I, which in turn led to World War II, was the assassination of Archduke Franz Ferdinand of Austria and his wife Sophia by seventeen-year-old Gavrilo Princip, a Serbian nationalist. The year was 1914. The place was Sarajevo, the capital of Bosnia-Hercegovina. Medjugorje is in Bosnia-Hercegovina! In short, the Queen of Peace came to Yugoslavia because she is warning us of another great war to come if the world continues in its present path of sin, degeneration, and destruction.

And so, this Mother of all Nations and Queen of Peace has been appearing daily in Medjugorje ever since 1981, but rather than paraphrase them, I prefer to quote some of her messages over the years exactly as she has given them, but not necessarily in the given sequence. She said:

> "Dear children, today I invite you to peace. I have come here as the Queen of Peace, and I desire to enrich you with my motherly peace. I love you and I desire to bring all of you to the peace which God gives and which enriches every heart. These days while I am with you are days of grace. I am with you and I desire to help you with my prayers and to guide you on the path of peace. Throughout the whole world there is lack of peace, therefore I call you to build up a new world of peace together with me by means of prayer.

> "Many people now live without faith. Some do not even want to hear about Jesus, but they still want peace and satisfaction! There is no peace when there is no prayer, and there is no love when there is no faith. People are attracted by many things and they forget about the more important things. At this time peace is threatened in a special way and I am asking you to renew prayer and fasting in your families. Dear children, I want you to grasp the seriousness of this situation. This is the reason why I need your prayers. Prayer is the only way to save the human race.

> "Pray, because Satan wants to destroy my plan of peace. Be reconciled with one another and, by means

of your lives, work so that peace may reign in the whole earth. Your mother is warning you that he is at work. I would like you to pay special attention to the fact that Satan is at work in a special way with young people. Persevere in praying the Rosary. The Rosary itself can achieve miracles in the world and in your life. The Rosary is not an ornament for the home, as one oftentimes would limit himself to using it. Tell everyone to pray it. I also call on you to read the Bible every day in your homes and let it be in a visible place to encourage you to read it and to pray.

"Excuse me for this, but you must realize that Satan exists. One day he appeared before the throne of God and asked permission to submit the Church to a period of trial. God gave him permission to try the Church for one century. This century is under the power of the devil, but when the secrets that are confided in you come to pass, his power would be destroyed. Even now he is beginning to lose his power and has become aggressive. He is destroying marriages, creating divisions among priests and is responsible for obsessions and murder. You must protect yourself against these things through fasting and prayer, especially community prayer. Carry blessed objects with you. Put them in your house and restore the use of holy water.

"I wish to tell you that I am with you even in these turbulent days when Satan wants to destroy all that I and my Son Jesus are building up. In particular he wants to destroy your souls. He wants to lead you away as far as possible from Christian living, and away from the commandments by which the Church is calling you to live. Satan wants to destroy all that is holy in you and around you. He wants war, wants lack of peace, wants to destroy all that is good. He is strong and wishes not only to destroy human life but also nature and the planet on which you live. Yes, Satan is indeed strong and is waiting to test each one of you, but if you pray, he cannot injure you even a little, because you are God's children and he is watching over you.

"The majority of people go to purgatory. Many go to hell. Only a small number go *directly* to heaven. In purgatory there are different levels. The lowest is close to hell and the highest gradually draws near heaven. There are in purgatory, souls who pray ardently to God, but for whom no relative or friend prays on earth, however, God makes them benefit from the prayers of other people. Therefore, little children, I am calling you today to the prayer of consecration to Jesus, my dear Son, so that each of your hearts may be his. And then I am calling you to consecration to my Immaculate Heart. I want you to consecrate yourselves, as persons, families, and parishes, so that all will belong to God through my hands.

"I particularly protect those who have been consecrated to me. Unceasingly adore the Most Blessed Sacrament of the altar. I am always present when the faithful are adoring. My Son, Jesus Christ, also wishes to bestow on you special graces through me. Seek from God the graces which he is giving you through me. Do not forget to seek because God has permitted me to obtain graces for you. If you wish that I be your protector, then confide in me all your intentions so that I can dispose of them according to the will of God.

"I wish to tell you that I have chosen this parish (Medjugorje) and that I am guarding it in my hands like a little flower that does not want to die. This parish, which I have chosen, is special and different from others, and I have given great graces to all who pray from the heart. Dear children, once again I desire to call you to prayer. When you pray, you are much more beautiful, like flowers, which, after the snow, show all their beauty and all their colors become indescribable. So, you, dear children, after prayer, are so much more beautiful before God. Therefore, pray and open your inner self to the Lord so that he makes of you a harmonious and beautiful flower for Paradise.

"You cannot imagine what is going to happen or what the Eternal Father will send to earth. That is why you must be converted. My wish is just to warn you all as a mother. I want to tell you how I suffer for all because I am the mother of all (nations). Let me be your mother and your tie to God. Renounce everything. Do penance. I beseech you, pray to Jesus. I am his mother, and I intercede for you with him. But all prayers go to Jesus. I will help, I will pray, but everything does not depend solely on me, but also on your strength, and on the strength of those who pray.

"Tell the priests, tell everyone, that it is you who are divided on earth. Love your Serbian, Orthodox and Muslim brothers. You are all my children. Certainly, all religions are not equal, but all men are equal before God. It does not suffice to belong to the Catholic Church to be saved, but it is necessary to respect the commandments of God in following one's conscience. Those who are not Catholics are no less creatures made in the image of God and destined to be rejoined someday to the House of the Father. Salvation is available to everyone without exception. Only those who refuse God deliberately are condemned. To him who has been given little, little would be asked for and to whomever has been given very much, very much would be required. It is God alone, in his infinite justice, who determines the degree of responsibility and pronounces his judgement.

"Many pretend to see Jesus and me and to understand our words but they are, in fact, lying. This is a very grave sin, and it is necessary to pray to him for them. I have come to call the world to conversion for the last time. Afterwards, I would not appear anymore on this earth. There are many people who do not desire to understand my messages or accept with seriousness what I am saying. But you are therefore called and asked that by your lives and your daily living you give witness to my presence. If you pray, God will help you discover the true reason for my coming. Therefore, little children, pray and read the Sacred Scriptures so that through my coming, you will discover the message in Sacred Scripture for you. The most important thing in your spiritual life is to ask for the gift of the Holy Spirit. When the Holy Spirit comes, then peace will be established."

Chapter 24

The Fourth Marian Dogma – The Assumption of the Blessed Virgin Mary

Scripture does not speak of Mary as having died or not having died. However, in the early days of the Church there was strong belief in the bodily Assumption of the Blessed Virgin Mary, and Fathers of the Church in the East and West preached homilies commemorating the Assumption with a directness which leaves no doubt as to their faith.

Now, it is necessary to keep in mind what the Assumption is not. Some people think that Catholics believe that Mary "ascended" into heaven. This is not correct. Christ, by his own power, ascended into heaven. However, Mary was assumed or taken up into heaven by God. She did not do it under her own power.

In the homily of Theoteknos (he ruled between 560 and 650 AD) of Livias (on the left bank of the Jordan), he speaks of the feast of the Assumption: "If the God-bearing body of Saint Mary has known death," he says, "it has not, nevertheless, suffered corruption; it has been preserved from corruption and kept free from stain and it has been raised to heaven with her pure, spotless soul by the holy angels and powers." "It was fitting," he says later, "that the most holy body of Mary, the God-bearing body, the receptacle of God, divinised, incorruptible, illuminated by divine grace and full of glory … should be entrusted to the earth for a little while and raised up to heaven in glory, with her soul pleasing to God."

About 50 years later, the feast was introduced in Rome and was mentioned in the papal decree of Pope Sergius I (687–701 AD), who fixed a procession for the feast. The Orthodox Church also celebrates the feast. According to the teaching on Mary in the Coptic Orthodox Church, the Lord did not permit the body in which he himself had dwelt and from which he had formed his own humanity to become a prey to corruption. St. Mary was a human being, her body died but was taken up to heaven. In fact, by the 8th century the Assumption was fully accepted in the East. However, while the Orthodox Church also professes the doctrine of the bodily Assumption of Mary, it has not defined it as a dogma.

The feast of the Assumption of the Blessed Virgin Mary is commemorated in the West on August 15. In the Coptic Church it is celebrated on August 22. The Ethiopian Orthodox Church, often referred to as the daughter of the Coptic Church, received the faith from Alexandria, and with it a great love for Mary. In fact, the Ethiopian hymnology to Mary is very numerous and rich, and they celebrate her Assumption not once a year, but monthly!

Between 1849 and 1950, numerous petitions for the doctrine to be made dogma arrived in Rome. They came from 113 Cardinals, 18 Patriarchs, 2,505 Archbishops, 32,000 priests, 50,000 religious women, and 8,000,000 lay people. On May 1, 1946, the Pope had sent to the bishops of the world the encyclical *Deiparae Virginis,* putting this question to them: "Most especially, we wish to know if you, Venerable Brethren, with your learning and prudence consider that the bodily Assumption of the Immaculate Blessed Virgin can be proposed and defined as a dogma of Faith and whether in addition to your own wishes this is desired by your clergy and people." When the replies were collated, it was found that 22 bishops out of 1,181 dissented but only 6 doubted that the Assumption was revealed truth. The other 16 simply questioned the opportuneness.

On November 1, 1950, by the Apostolic Constitution *Munificentissimus Deus,* Pope Pius XII defined the Assumption of Our Lady as a dogma of faith. He gave the reasons for this singular honour: "From all eternity the Mother of God is united in a mysterious way to Jesus Christ. Immaculate in her conception, a spotless virgin in her divine motherhood, the noble companion of the Redeemer who won a complete triumph over sin and its consequences, she finally obtained as a crowning glory of her privileges, preservation from the corruption of the tomb and was raised body and soul into the glory of heaven."

Theologically, the corruption of the body is a consequence of the corruption of original sin. But Mary was exempted from the corruption of original sin and it was most fitting therefore that she should be exempted from corruption of the grave. In short, the Assumption is really a consequence of the Immaculate Conception. And as Pius XII also said: "These two singular privileges bestowed upon the Mother of God stand out in a most splendid light at the beginning and the end of her earthly journey."

As Alphonse Bossard said: "Her Divine Motherhood is in utter harmony with her Assumption, as are her Immaculate Conception and perpetual virginity. How could the body of her in whom 'the Word was made flesh' to save the flesh have known the corruption of the grave? Or the body of her who totally escaped the power of sin? And the body of her, who by her virginal consecration, belonged to her Son and his mission in a perfect and exclusive way?"

Dealing with Scripture, the Apostolic Constitution does not appeal directly to any one text as conclusive evidence of the truth. However, some express the view that the dogma is contained in Revelation 12 in an implicit manner: "Now a great sign appeared in heaven: a woman clothed with the sun, standing on the moon, and with twelve stars on her head for a crown" (Rev. 12:1).

However, the doctrine of the Assumption does not specify if Mary died. It merely states that after the completion of her life, she was taken body and soul into heaven. Elijah and Enoch were assumed into heaven without dying, just as the righteous will be at the end of time (Genesis 5:24; 2 Kings 2:11; I Thess. 4:17; Hebrews 11:5). Why then is it hard to believe that God gave his mother this privilege? Matthew 27:52 suggests a bodily assumption before the Second Coming, and most Protestants believe in the "rapture" based on the events described in 1 Thess. 4:17 and 1 Cor. 15:52. And so, some argue that Mary is simply the first to be "raptured."

Indeed, no city has ever claimed her body and there is no record of her relics or remains anywhere. Rome, for example, claims the tombs of Peter and Paul. Peter's tomb is under the High Altar of the Basilica that bears his name. Other cities have claimed the remains of other saints, and we know that the bones of some saints were distributed to several cities. We also know that after the Crucifixion, Mary was cared for by the apostle John, and it is believed he went to live in Ephesus and that Mary accompanied him there. Scripture is silent on this, however. There is some dispute about where she ended her life, perhaps there, perhaps back in Jerusalem. Nonetheless, it is interesting that neither of those cities or any other has claimed her remains. Remember that in the early 15th century relics of saints were jealously guarded, highly prized. Here was Mary, certainly the most privileged of all the saints, but we have no records of her bodily remains being venerated anywhere. This certainly lends support to her assumption.

That Scripture omits to record the fact is no argument against it. Omission is not denial. Here, of course, we get into the entirely separate matter, the question of *sola scriptura*. Indeed, the Bible actually denies that it is the complete rule of faith. John tells us not everything concerning Christ's work is in the Scriptures (John 21: 25), and Paul says that much Christian teaching is to be found in the tradition that is handed down by word of mouth (2 Timothy 2:2).

And so, the papal definition does not take a position on whether the Virgin Mary died and was assumed into heaven afterward or was transformed without going through death. It remains a question that theologians may freely debate. However, the opinion that Mary, like her Son, passed through death in order to be raised up, immediately or after a short interval, has by far the strongest support in tradition. For although she was holy, innocent, and never committed a sin, it is believed that she died in order to be in union with Jesus. Jesus chose to die. In this regard she also accepted death as Jesus accepted death.

But what did the Protestant reformers have to say? On the issue of the Assumption, Luther does not speak precisely but is content to assert on August 15, 1522, the feast of the Assumption: "From this gospel one cannot draw any conclusion about the fashion in which Mary is in heaven. It is not necessary any more, to know the fate of the saints in heaven. It is enough to know that they dwell in Christ as God says in Matthew 22:32; 'God is not a God of the dead but of the living.'"

Bullinger, the successor of the Swiss Reformer Zwingli, wrote in 1565: "The most learned theologians say that one cannot assert anything on the matter of the Assumption of the Virgin. To wish to unearth or clarify certain facts on which Scripture is silent is not without its dangers. Let us content ourselves with believing that the Virgin Mary is indeed active in heaven and has received every beatitude after her departing."

However, in 1568 he wrote on the same subject: "Elijah was transported body and soul in a chariot of fire. He was not buried in any church bearing his name, but mounted up to heaven so that on the one hand we might know what immortality and recompense God prepares for his faithful prophets and his most outstanding and incomparable creatures, and on the other hand in order to withdraw from men the possibility of venerating the human body of the saints. It is for this reason, we believe, that the pure and immaculate embodiment of the Mother of God, the Virgin Mary, the Temple of the Holy Spirit, that is to say, her saintly body, was carried up into heaven by the angels."

But St. Catherine Labouré certainly confirmed that on the night of July 18, 1830. When she was led into the chapel in the Rue du Bac in Paris at 11:30 p.m. by the angel, believed to be her guardian angel, "she heard a noise like the rustle of a silk dress." She looked toward the direction of the sound, and saw a lady descending the altar steps. The lady seated herself in the Director's chair, then, to quote the nun's own words, "looking upon the Blessed Virgin, I flung myself towards her, and falling upon my knees on the altar steps, I rested my hands on her lap." The lap obviously felt solid!

Catherine died on December 31, 1876. Pope Pius XI beatified her in 1933, and Pope Pius XII declared her a saint on July 27, 1947. Her incorrupt body still lies in the chapel of the Rue du Bac in Paris.

Eighteen years after the Blessed Virgin appeared to Catherine Labouré, she appeared in Lourdes to Bernadette Soubirous, and said: "I am the Immaculate Conception." She was sinless and, therefore, like her Son, was preserved from the corruption of the grave.

So the Church teaches. But the Virgin left us another hint of that. She, who was chosen by her to deliver the message of the Immaculate Conception, was herself given the privilege of incorruptibility. On two occasions I visited the convent of St. Gildard in Nevers, France, wherein lies the incorrupt body of St. Bernadette in a glass casket behind the altar rail. If the messenger of the Queen was given that privilege by God, surely, Her Majesty must have had a similar privilege and in a more perfect way.

Chapter 25

Disunity Among the Religions

According to Joseph Jared, the author of *What The Great Religions Believe,* as far as can be determined, religion has always existed in every society, from the most primitive to the most culturally advanced. The more keys which modern science finds with which to open the locked doors of the past, and the more we learn about the early days of men on earth, the more evidence there is that all the societies in the past had some form of religion, and the worship of some form of god. However, there is disunity among the religions of today and the one religion established by Yahweh in the Old Testament has been fractured. The Church is divided.

Judaism

Judaism is the religion of the Jewish people, and it was the first great faith to hold that there is only one God. It originated about 4,000 years ago with a Chalcean man named Abraham, who left his country of pagan worship, the land of Ur. This monotheism of Judaism is reflected in the *Shema* (the name): "Hear, O Israel, the Lord our God, the Lord is one" (Deuteronomy 6:4). This verse is the credo of the Jewish religion and begins every service in every Jewish synagogue throughout the world.

Now, in the Bible there is emphasis on the Jews being God's chosen people: "… The Lord thy God has chosen you to be a people for his own possession, out of all the peoples that are on the face of the earth" (Deuteronomy 7:6). "Chosen," however, means a people accepting a covenant to be God's witnesses and evangelists, but does not, generally speaking, in any way mean superiority.

Moses was given the Ten Commandments by Yahweh on Mount Sinai. It was a code of life, and the Ten Commandments became the core of the Five Books of the Old Testament, the Pentateuch. These five books, the first part of Hebrew Scriptures, known as the Torah, are often referred to as the Law, and Jewish tradition credits Moses with the authorship of these books. Indeed, in Hebrew history Moses is to Judaism as Christ is to Christianity and Muhammed is to Islam.

However, Judaism does not accept that Jesus is the Son of God. Indeed, the Christian belief in Jesus as the Son of God appears to many Jews as something entirely "unJewish," and they consider the doctrine of the Trinity to be polytheism and an absolute contradiction to the strict monotheism of Judaism.

Judaism also rejects original sin and believes that man enters the world free of sin with a soul that is pure, innocent and untainted. There is also belief in the immortality of the soul, in the resurrection of the dead at the end of time, and in the final judgment, teaching that if a man was evil his soul descends to hell (Gehennah) where punishment is meted out for sins committed, and when cleansed of all sins, purified souls ascend to heaven.

Throughout the turbulent history of the Jewish people, the belief in the coming of a personal Messiah has been an integral part of their faith. The Messianic hope was that the Messiah, a son of David, having defeated their enemies, would restore Israel to its former glory and reconcile the people to God. His Jewish opponents and many people who had first hoped that Jesus would be the Messiah who would deliver them from the Roman yoke and restore Israel to the glory of Davidic times, became disillusioned with him when they realized that he was not interested in military power but in their religious transformation. He was not therefore the kind of Messiah they had expected.

And so, Judaism is still awaiting that Messiah and does not believe, as Christians do, that Jesus was that person, neither do they believe that he resurrected from the dead. According to Moses Maimonides (1135–1224), said to be the greatest Jewish teacher of that age, "the Messiah will come, even if he is delayed."

Christianity

Christianity is the faith which has the largest following in the world and it is estimated that there are about one billion Christians today. It began in Israel with the story of its founder, Jesus of Nazareth. Christianity therefore sprung from Judaism, and he who encounters Jesus, encounters Judaism, for according to his human nature, Jesus was a Jew. All Christians firmly believe that Jesus is the Son of God and that his miracles are some of the prophetic signs of his divinity. As a consequence of this, the shared beliefs of Judaism and Christianity stop at the Old Testament.

Christianity, like Judaism, believes in the immortality of the soul, in heaven and hell and in the resurrection of the body. However, Roman Catholicism also teaches that there is a Purgatory where some souls are cleansed from the effects of unforgiven venial sins and endure temporal punishment for sins already forgiven before eventually going to heaven.

Unlike Judaism, however, Christianity believes in the doctrine of original sin and the need for baptism. At the age of thirty John the Baptist baptized Jesus. This event reminds me of a quip of Fr. Bruno Hussar, a Dominican priest, who related that one day while speaking to an Arab Christian friend, he happened to remind him that Jesus was a Jew, whereupon his friend explained: "Yes, but after he was baptized by John, he became a Christian!" Indeed, in the first two decades after the death of Jesus, all Christian converts came mostly from the Jews. Eventually, since many of them would not embrace Christianity, the Jewish convert Paul took the faith to the Gentiles. And so, one may say that with respect to religion the Jordan River separates the Jews from the Christians.

A crucial Christian concept, the mystery of the Trinity, holds that while God is fully one, he is also three: "The Father and I are one," said Jesus (John 10:30), but he also spoke of a third party in the Godhead: "I have said these things to you while still with you, but the Advocate, the Holy Spirit, whom the Father will send in my name, will teach you everything and remind you of all I had said to you" (John 14:25-26). And in his last commission given to his apostles, he groups these three persons of the Godhead into a single statement: "Go, therefore, make disciples of all *nations*; baptize them in the name of the Father, and of the Son, and of the Holy Spirit" (Matthew 28:19-20).

A most central act of worship performed by the early Christians and certain Christian churches to this day is the celebration of the Eucharist, the transubstantiation of bread and wine into the body and blood of Christ at the Consecration during the celebration of the Mass. Indeed, this is the backbone of the Roman Catholic and Orthodox Churches.

Islam

Islam is the youngest of the world's three major religions and originated in the 7th century AD. It is estimated that there are about 850 million Muslims in the world today. Its conceptual roots are in Judaism and Christianity. Muhammed is the founder of Muhammedanism or Islam, the preferred title. He was born into the leading tribe of Mecca, the Koerish, in approximately 571 AD. Islam was born in the desert region of Arabia and at that time was considered an "Arab religion for the Arabs," just as Judaism was the religion of the Jews many centuries before.

Muhammed is considered to be a prophet like Moses, who guided the Arabs towards monotheistic truth, but today the vast majority of Muslims are not Arabs. Indeed, the three biggest Muslim nations are Indonesia (about 160 million Muslims), Pakistan (about 100 million), and Bangladesh with 90 million. But as many as 140 million Muslims live in sub-Saharan Africa. According to Muslim tradition, the Koran is the infallible word of God revealed to the Prophet Muhammed by the angel Gabriel. Unlike Jesus, Muhammed had no miraculous powers and when asked by his fellow citizens to show them a miracle which would prove his right to claim the gift of prophecy, he confidently appealed to the Koran itself. The miracle, he said, was the Koran.

Muslims see their religion as a continuation and *rectification* of the Judeo-Christian tradition, and the Jewish Scriptures and the prophetic mission of Jesus are incorporated by reference in the Koran. The Koran teaches that God, the same God known to the Arabians as Allah, favoured Jews and Christians by revealing his truth to them in Holy Books, but they deviated from what was revealed and fell into error and corruption.

The creed of Islam consists in a single sentence: "There is no God but Allah, and Muhammed is his Prophet." The word Allah is from the prefix a*l* meaning *"the"* and *Illah* meaning *"God."* The word Allah therefore literally means "the God." Like Judaism, Islam rejects the doctrine of the Trinity and the divinity of Jesus. In Islam's eyes Christians have compromised their monotheism by deifying Christ. And so, Islam honours Jesus as a true Prophet of God, but not as the Son of God. It even accepts the Christian doctrine of his virgin birth. But of the doctrine of the Incarnation and the Trinity, it draws the line, seeing these as concessions to man's inclination to seek a compromise between the human and divine. But the Christian Bible quotes the same angel Gabriel as saying: "And so, the child will be holy and be called Son of God" (John 1:35-36)!

The Koran also says that Jesus was not crucified but was taken up into heaven by God after another who resembled him was killed in his place (Koran 4:157). Islam, therefore, by rejecting the incarnation and the death of Jesus on the Cross rejects altogether all ideas of the redemption of man, the sole purpose of the incarnation of Christ as taught in the Christian religion.

As Pope John Paul II says in his book *Crossing the Threshold of Hope:* "There is no room for the Cross and the Resurrection (in Islam). Jesus is mentioned, but only as a prophet who prepares for the last prophet, Muhammed. There is also mention of Mary, his virgin mother, but the tragedy of redemption is completely absent. For this reason not only the theology but also the anthropology of Islam is very distant from Christianity."

Because Islam does not espouse the doctrine of original sin, there is also no rite of baptism. Islam, however, like Judaism and Christianity, admits to the doctrine of the resurrection of the body and retributions according to works. It believes that depending on how the soul fares that soul will go to either heaven or hell. In fact, the Koran's description of the torments of hell are very vivid.

In its description of heaven the Koran says: "As for the righteous, they shall be lodged in peace together amidst gardens and fountains, arrayed in rich silks and fine brocade. Yes, and We shall wed them to dark-eyed houris" (Koran 44:43). But Christianity quotes Christ as saying: "The children of this world take wives and husbands, but those who are judged worthy of a place in the other world and in the resurrection from the dead do not marry because they can no longer die, for they are the same as the angels, and being children of the resurrection they are sons of God" (Luke 20:35-37).

In the Old Testament polygamy was accepted at one stage but Judaism eventually prohibited it. It is also not permitted in Christianity. The Koran, on the other hand, authorizes polygamy up to four simultaneous wives if the wives agree to it and if the man is willing to treat his wives equally, both on an emotional and a material basis. After the death of Khadija, Muhammed's first wife, Muhammed himself had nine wives. However, with the westernization of the Muslim world and on account of the laws of many countries, polygamy today is uncommon.

On Religious Intermarriage

The Book of Kings records that King Solomon married many foreign wives "from those peoples of whom Yahweh had said to the Israelites, 'You shall not enter into marriage with them, neither shall they with you; for they will surely incline your heart'" (1 Kings 11:2). Indeed, the Bible also says: "When Solomon was old, his wives turned away his heart after other gods; and his heart was not true to the Lord his God, as was the heart of his father David" (1 Kings 11:4).

Today's religious Jews still oppose intermarriage for those same reasons that motivate the devout of all faiths. Rabbi Morris Ketzer in his book *What Is A Jew* states: "Differences in religion between husband and wife present a serious obstacle to a truly harmonious relationship; such marriages, even when they endure, impose a constant strain on the religious loyalties of both partners, and raise serious personal and family problems difficult to solve."

As for Islam, a Koranic injunction against marriage to unbelievers has meant, in legal practice, that Muslim men may marry Muslim women or women from among the "people of the book" (Christians and Jews), but they may not marry pagans. On the other hand, Muslim women may only marry Muslim men. However, this is not strictly observed today.

The Christian churches likewise prefer intermarriage among Christians, but the Catholic Church, for example, accepts such marriages provided that the children are brought up in the Catholic faith. According to the *Catechism of the Catholic Church* (1994): "Marriage between a Catholic and a baptized non-Catholic requires particular attention on the part of couples and their pastors. A case of marriage with disparity of cult (between a Catholic and a non-baptized person) requires even greater circumspection." It goes on to state that "the difficulties of mixed marriages must not be underestimated. The spouses risk experiencing the tragedy of Christian disunity even in the heart of their own home. Disparity of cult can further aggravate these difficulties. Differences about faith and the very notion of marriage, but also different religious mentalities can become sources of tension in a marriage, especially as regards to education of their children. The temptation to religious indifference can then arise."

This indeed has been the exact stand of Pope Leo XIII (1878–1903). In one of his Encyclicals, he wrote: "Care also must be taken that they (Catholics) do not easily enter into marriage to those who are not Catholics; for when minds do not agree as to the observances of religion, it is scarcely possible to hope for agreement in other things.... They give occasion to forbidden association and communion in religious matters; endanger the faith of the Catholic partner; are a hindrance to the proper education of their children, and often lead to a mixing up of truth and falsehood, and to the belief that all religions are equally as good."

All will be one

And so, the three major world religions have major differences in their beliefs. Indeed, even within the main religions there are splits and factions. For example, although it is very clear in Scripture and early Church history that Jesus Christ left only *one* Church, today there are over 20,000 denominations within that Church. But God is truth and truth cannot contradict itself. The day must therefore soon come when the truth, the whole truth, and nothing but the truth will be revealed and all will believe in the one truth.

In Medjugorje (not yet officially approved by the Church), the Blessed Virgin is claimed to have told the visionaries: "I am the mother of all." Then she later went on to say: "In God there are no divisions, but you men have made divisions.… You have to esteem all men, no matter to what religion they belong. In many places you deprecate people who belong to other religions. This is not good. God does not want this. God wants you to love all and that you esteem all."

On another occasion, as recorded by Fr. Svetozar Kraljevic in his book *The Apparitions of Our Lady at Medjugorje,* the Virgin is also quoted as saying: "It is not equally efficacious to belong to or pray in any church or community because the Holy Spirit grants his power differently among the churches and ministers. Moreover, all believers do not pray the same way." It is intentional that all apparitions are under the auspices of the Catholic Church. She then prophesied that "in the end all will be one."

Pope John Paul II, in his encyclical *Redemptoris Missio* (Mission of the Redeemer), warns against an attitude that "one religion is as good as another," and in his chapter on *Why So Many Religions?* in his book *Crossing the Threshold of Hope,* he writes: "The Council remarks that: 'The Catholic Church rejects nothing that is true and holy in these (other) religions. The Church has a high regard for their conduct and way of life, for those precepts and doctrines which, although differing on many points from that which the Church believes and propounds, often reflect a ray of that truth which enlightens all men.'

"However, the Church proclaims, and is bound to proclaim that Christ is *'the way and the truth and the life'* (John 4:6) in whom men must find the fullness of religious life and in whom God has reconciled everything to himself (*Nostra Aetate* 2) … Christ came into the world for all *nations.* He redeemed them all and has his own ways of reaching each of them in the present eschatological phase of salvation history."

And in the chapter *In Search of Lost Unity,* he says: "Christians are more deeply aware that the divisions existing between them are contrary to Christ's prayer at the Last Supper: 'that they may all be one, as you, Father, are in me and I in you … that the world may believe that you sent me' (John 17:21) … He (Christ) founded only one Church — the only one capable of speaking in his name.… These divisions are certainly opposed to what Christ had in mind.

"It is impossible to imagine that this Church, instituted by Christ on the foundation of the apostles and of Peter, should not be one.… By the year 2000 we need to be more united, more willing to advance along the path toward the unity for which Christ prayed on the eve of his Passion. This unity is enormously precious. In a certain sense, the future of the world is at stake. The future of the Kingdom of God in the world is at stake."

Chapter 26

Next Year in Jerusalem

Four times have I been to Jerusalem and each time I have been awed by its mystique and by the plaintive chants of the Old City. At the wailing wall there are the Hasidic rabbis, their sidecurls swinging as they pray: *"Shma Yisrael* (Hear, O Israel). *Adonai Eloheinu* (The Lord our God). *Adonai Ehad* (The Lord is one)." Then deep inside the Holy Sepulchre a few hundred yards away, the air is laden with incense from an Armenian service, and then Franciscan monks follow the Armenians, taking their places at a small altar and singing: "Christ has died. Christ has risen. Christ will come again." Outside can be heard the chants of the Muslims' call to prayer from loud speakers on *Al-Aqsa,* the Muslim mosque: *"Allahu akbar* (God is most great)! *La ilaha illa Allah* (There is no god but God)."

The name of Jerusalem in Hebrew is, ironically, *Yerushalayim* ("City of Peace"). In Arabic it is *Al-Quds* ("The Holy"). Its beginnings are lost in the midst of antiquity, but it was already there (called Salem) when Abraham the Patriarch arrived in the Promised Land and accepted "bread and wine" from its Canaanite king, Melchizedek, nearly 4,000 years ago. All through a succession of conquerors and rulers from King David, who captured it in 1010 BC, how often has Jerusalem been pagan, Christian or Muslim? How many different conquerors have wielded their power over it? — Jebusites, Egyptians, Babylonians, Prussians, Greeks and Romans, Muslim Arabs, Seljuks, Fatimids, Crusaders, Mamelukes, Ottoman Turks, British, Jordanians, and now again, the Israelites!

Jewish attachment to Jerusalem, where they all lived under King David and built their first temple under King Solomon, has remained a source of abiding faith after they were crushed, enslaved and exiled into Babylon in 587 BC. Throughout all the centuries of their exile, from the farthest corners of the earth Jews have prayed for their return to Jerusalem: "Next year in Jerusalem!" History has no parallel to this mystic bond. There they sang and dreamed of returning to the Holy City, and from there they did return to build and restore. Under Herod they re-erected their temple, which survived until the Romans destroyed it by fire in 70 AD on a day still mourned by Jews. It was the prophecy of Jesus: "You see all these? I tell you solemnly, not a single stone here will be left on another: everything will be destroyed" (Matthew 24:1-3).

For close to 3,000 years, the Jews did not have a country of their own. Great nations of the pagan era which appeared at the same time the Jews did have totally disappeared. The Babylonians, the Persians, the Phoenicians, the Hittites, and the Philistines have all vanished from the face of the earth after once having been great and mighty powers. The Chinese, the Hindus in India, and the Egyptian peoples are as old as the Jewish people. However, unlike the Jews, they were never driven out of their countries, nor did they face the problem of survival in alien lands. The Jews, however, survived 3,000 years without a country of their own, yet they preserved their ethnic identity among alien cultures.

They made memory a part of a ritual, holding their devotion to Jerusalem as the city changed hands again and again in blood, as Muslim conquerors were ejected by the Crusaders in 1099, and then in turn they drove out the Crusaders in 1187. Indeed, the Muslims, through the Ottoman Turks, held Jerusalem until the end of World War I in 1917 when the British took over and set the stage for the re-establishment of the Jewish nation.

Not until Zionism evolved as a movement in the 19th century, largely in reaction to pogroms in Russia, did significant numbers of European Jews begin to migrate to Ottoman-controlled Palestine. By 1845, Jews formed the largest single community in Jerusalem, the vanguard of an influx that gathered momentum after Great

Britain endorsed the creation of a Jewish homeland through the Balfour Declaration of 1917.

The migration gained urgency as Hitler came to power, promulgated anti-Jewish laws in Germany in the 1930s, then rounded up Jews in Germany, deported them to concentration camps and exterminated an estimated 6 million of them in the cause of ethnic purity. Out of this holocaust grew the international compassion for the proposal of a new Israel as a sanctuary for the Jews, and the historic decision by the United Nations General Assembly in November 1947 to partition Palestine was passed by a vote of thirty three in favour, thirteen against, and ten in abstention.

They had waited a long time for their return — 19 centuries. For generations they had repeated the words of Ezekiel: "Thus says the Lord God, I will gather you from the peoples, and assemble you out of the countries where you have been scattered and I will give you the land of Israel" (Ezekiel 11:17) and the prophecy of the prophet Jeremiah: "Thus said the Lord of hosts, the God of Israel: Yet again shall they use this speech in the land of Judah and the cities thereof, when I shall bring again their captivity" (Jeremiah 31:23). Indeed, the reconstitution of Hebrew as a living national language is one of the miracles of our day.

The ingathering, however, was not achieved without stresses and strains, heartaches, and bitter disappointments. During those early years, if there was not enough to eat or the water supply stopped functioning, or the electric power failed, the Israelis would half-facetiously blame the occurrence on "the ingathering of the exiles." For example, a stoic joke in those days was: "For 2,000 years we Jews have been hoping and fighting and praying for the return — and it had to happen to me!"

Scarcely more than a dot on the map in the Middle East, surrounded by enemies with large territories, it is scarred and coveted by both the Jews and Arabs, who now face each other in a family feud, for the Jews and Arabs are cousins. About 3.5 million Jews and 2 million Arabs live in Israel, but both peoples are victims. Each has suffered at the hands of outsiders, and each has been wounded by the other. But as David Shipler wrote in his book *Arab and Jew,* the hardships of the Palestinians in modern history bear no resemblance in scope and depth to those of the Jews. Subjected to Turkish brutality under the Ottoman Empire, British rule under the Mandate created by the League of Nations, political unrest by the Jordanian monarchy, and tough controls under Israel, the Arabs from this crucial slice of Palestine have suffered powerlessness and deprivation of liberty, but never genocide.

The Palestinian awakening was heightened by the upheavals of Israel's birth in 1948 and the refusal of the Arab governments to accept the presence of the tiny Jewish state on the edge of Arab territory. The patterns of war that followed that statehood in 1948, 1956, 1967, 1973, and 1982 gave license to hatred and ground to extremists on both sides. As a result, many Palestinian Arabs have been the victims of expulsions, displacement and war. Ironically, they have also found themselves scattered and rejected in their own Arab world at large, excluded from full participation in the countries where many have settled and were confined at one time to squalid refugee camps. And so, while the Palestinians are part of the Arab majority in the region, they are also a minority subgroup in the Arab world.

The Arab exodus from Palestine is the 12th largest movement of refugees to take place since the end of World War II. The India-Pakistan conflict, for example, led to 2,388,000 Muslims moving from India into Pakistan and 2,644,000 Hindus moving from Pakistan to India. When Vietnam was partitioned, 800,000 North Vietnamese moved to the South. In Korea the same thing happened with approximately the same numbers involved.

But according to Genesis, this was the land that God gave to Abraham and his seed, and some of the Jews of modern Israel have therefore articulated their biblical claim to Israel on this biblical promise, readily disregarding the centuries of Muslim rule that followed. On the other hand, those Arabs who regard history as their ally tend to begin with the Muslim conquest in the seventh century AD, and the fact that they were the majority of the population in the country at the end of World War I, while blithely ignoring the Jewish kingdoms that existed there 2,000 years before Mohammed made his appearance.

But in at least three respects Jerusalem differs from most other places. The city is holy to the adherents of three religions. It is the subject of conflicting national claims by two peoples, and its population is heterogeneous to a considerable degree. In the Holy See's view, the historical and material characteristics of this city, as well as its religious and cultural characteristics, must be preserved. The rights of freedom of religion and worship and of access for residents and pilgrims alike, whether from the Holy Land itself or from other parts of the world, must be safeguarded. Israelis and Palestinians, in the desired search for a political settlement of their conflict over Jerusalem, cannot overlook the fact that the city has aspects which go far beyond their legitimate national interest. Indeed, the peace of the whole world is increasingly dependent upon the peace of Jerusalem.

As Pope John Paul II in his address to the Diplomatic Corps on January 11, 1992, said: "What a blessing it would be if this Holy Land, where God spoke and Jesus worked, could become a special place of encounter and prayer for people; if this Holy City of Jerusalem could be a sign and instrument of peace and reconciliation!" Indeed, it is in Jerusalem that Jesus was rejected, was crucified and rose again. From this city he ascended into heaven and to this city he will return. In the City of Jerusalem the first Christian community sprang up and remained throughout the centuries a continual ecclesial presence despite many difficulties. This was the place where he commissioned those Jewish apostles to go to every part of the world and proclaim the good news to every creature. It was here that the Jewish people fell and through that fall, salvation came to the Gentiles. It was from Jerusalem that they were dispersed in 70 AD throughout the whole world and it is to Jerusalem that they have now returned.

One may well ask what could have occasioned 1,900 years of exile and suffering but the rejection of the Messiah! At present they do not recognize him as their true glory, but in the end they would see him as a fulfillment of their history and the meaning of their destiny. It is believed that when the fullness of time has come, then the veil will be taken away from the hearts of the Jewish people and they would be grafted back.

Chapter 27

The World at War

There are many who believe that the Blessed Virgin Mary first appeared on June 21, 1981, to six young children in Medjugorje, Yugoslavia, and that she has continued to do so to this day. Medjugorje is in Bosnia-Hercegovina and its capital city is Sarajevo. She identified herself there as the Queen of Peace and is claimed to have said that these apparitions are her last in these times. Significantly, her title Queen of Peace is the last of the titles given to her in the Litany of Loreto. But like every one of her apparition sites, Yugoslavia was not haphazardly chosen by the Blessed Virgin Mary. She warned of war and in 1992, we saw the start of the most atrocious ethnic war since Hitler tried to establish Aryan superiority over the nations of the world. She said there that this 20th century is the century of Satan's last-ditch stand in the great battle between the woman and her seed and himself and his seed (Genesis 3:15).

But the history of the human race is one of war. As Winston Churchill once said: "Except for brief and precious interludes there has never been peace in the world, and long before history began murderous strife was universal and unending." Indeed, in the 17th century it is said that there were only seven calendar years without a major war between European states. The 18th century began with the wars of Louis XIV and ended with those of Napoleon, but in the 19th and 20th centuries wars were much more bloody and devastating as weaponry became more and more lethal.

World War I was expected to be over by Christmas of 1914, and conscripts enlisted by the hundreds of thousands, bursting with burgeoning nationalism. The nation was supreme. When it ended on November 11, 1918, over 10 million lives were lost, many more maimed. World War I also made possible the Russian Revolution in 1917 and greatly contributed to the great Depression of the thirties, the rise of communism, and the economic collapse which helped drive the Germans into Hitler's embrace. The rise of Adolph Hitler and the onset of World War II resulted from the humiliation of Germany and the imperfect peace that ended World War I.

Hitler's ultimatum to Poland finally pushed Britain and France over the edge. By the end of 1941, with the Japanese attack on Pearl Harbor, the war had become a truly global conflict. World War II had engulfed the world and it would prove to be the bloodiest conflict ever known in history. Fifty million people, including six million European Jews, would die before Berlin fell to the Soviet Red Army on May 8, 1945. In August of that year, the United States dropped two atomic bombs on Japan, ending the war and changing the world. It was the birth of the nuclear age. Hiroshima and Nagasaki were living hells. There were charred bodies all over the land and people were walking like ghosts with their skin peeled and hanging like seaweed.

But even as the guns fell silent in 1945, a new threat began to take shape. The defeat of the Nazis greatly strengthened Soviet Russia, which had borne a great brunt of the fighting. Soviet aggrandizement and Western resistance then triggered the "Cold War," which led to "hot wars," first in Korea, where 3 million people died, then in Vietnam, communist regimes in the North launched wars to capture by force the non-communist South countries at a cost of 1.5 million lives. Uneasy allies throughout the war, the Russians seemed bent on installing friendly regimes in the Eastern European lands which they had liberated. And so, the Iron Curtain descended, as Winston Churchill had prophesied.

Meanwhile in Algeria and other parts of Africa, colonialism was ended by wars of national liberation or by guerrilla movements, but the consequences were no less deadly. In the Balkans, bitter wars of ethnic identity developed and seriously threatened world stability and peace. There were also certain critical moments when America and the Soviet Union might have come in conflict — the Berlin blockade of 1948 and the Cuban missile crisis of 1962. However, sober heads on both sides devised alternatives to Armageddon.

But there were wars all over the world. When hard-line communist regimes collapsed, and we thought that freedom of religion and democracy would bring the world closer to God, they all seemed to do so in a similar way, a kind of gangster capitalism, with a cadre of Mafia elites and the emergence of corruption. It is the story of present-day Russia and other European communist countries. The murderous Khmer Rouge in Asia was no different. It was a sadistic revolution that left 1.7 million Cambodians dead. Now the red flag of so-called democratic Kampuchea has given way to the red lights of massage palours and brothels. It was the fleshpot legacy of Pol Pot.

There were other wars in the Central and South American continents, including Nicaragua, Argentina, Chile, Colombia, Peru, Cuba and San Salvador. In Africa, war erupted in Rwanda, Congo, Algeria, Angola, Uganda, Chad, Namibia, Zimbabwe, Burundi, Sudan, Eritrea, Ethiopia, Sierra Leone, and some other countries. There were ethnic and religious wars in Israel, Iran and Iraq, India, Indonesia, East Timor, Afghanistan, Sri Lanka, Northern Ireland, and in Bosnia and Kosovo in Yugoslavia. In this latter country, there has been an impious plenitude of callous murders, rapes, and destruction of houses and churches. Eleven thousand people died in Sarajevo. Two thousand were children. And so, the Balkan Peninsula is again nurturing conflicts that are centuries old. It is the arch-example of national and ethnic hatred and disunity. The nations are still at war. God's children are fighting each other.

Of this latest war in Kosovo, history records that on June 15, 1389, the Serb Knights of King Lazer I stood on Kosovo's rugged ground in a last-ditch effort to forestall the advancing Muslim Turks of Sultan Murad, but a humiliated Serbia eventually fell under Muslim control for centuries. According to the late Cambridge University historian C. W. Perevitie-Orton, the occupying Turks committed centuries of atrocities. Serbia then recaptured Kosovo from Turkey in 1913, but by then ethnic Albanians were a majority in the province. For Serbia, Kosovo's 1.8 million ethnic Albanian

Muslims — 90% of the population — are inexorably linked to the 14th century Ottoman invaders. The battle of Kosovo gave birth to Serbian nationalism and Serbia is now avenging that 600-year-old wound. As a Serb journalist conceded in an Italian newspaper: "We have gone back to primordial times."

Chapter 28

The Lady of
All Nations (PART II)

The apparitions of the *Lady, Mary, Mother of all Nations* began in Amsterdam on the feast of the Annunciation, March 25, 1945. Ida relates that she was in conversation with her sisters and her spiritual director Fr. J. Frehe just before the first apparition took place. To quote her testimony: "I felt drawn to the adjoining room. I suddenly saw a light and said to myself: 'Where is this light coming from? What a curious light?' The wall then disappeared before my eyes. There was instead one sea of light in an empty space, and out of it I suddenly saw a figure moving forward, a female figure.

"She was clad in white and wore a sash. She stood with her arms lowered and the palms of her hands turned outwards towards me. I thought it must be the Blessed Virgin and that it could not be anyone else. I then said: 'Are you Mary?' She answered: 'They will call me the Lady, Mother.' As she said it, there was a smile on her face (by that time her sisters had joined her in the room). I repeated what she said loudly and with that I heard Fr. Frehe say: 'Lady? Well, I never heard that before. The Lady!' The Lady lifted up three, then four, and finally five fingers. While doing this she said: 'The three represent March, the four, April, and the five is for the fifth of May.'"

Immediately afterwards she showed Ida the Rosary, and said: "It is thanks to this. Persevere (in saying it)." Then Ida saw a large crowd of soldiers, many of whom were soldiers of the Allies. The Lady said: "Now, these will soon return to their homes." After that she withdrew very slowly and only then did the light disappear and Ida saw everything around her in the room as it always had been.

As she had hinted with her five fingers, World War II ended in Holland on May 5, 1945! It was at that time the feast of Pope Pius V. Significantly, it was this Pope who rallied Christendom in Europe to storm heaven with Rosaries before the Battle of Lepanto, which was to decide the faith and fate of Europe, and which took place in 1571 near the Greek islands. The Islamic fleet vastly outnumbered the Christian fleet and the outcome was considered to be inevitable. However, through a miraculous gust of wind, the Islamic fleet was scattered in total disarray and Christianity won the day. The victory was attributed to the Rosary. The date was October 7, 1571, and to this day October 7 is celebrated as the feast of the Most Holy Rosary of the Blessed Virgin Mary.

During the second apparition on April 21, 1945, Ida was shown some scenes of the Old Testament. These were most unique in the history of Marian apparitions, and which I found to be most interesting. She first saw the exodus of the Jews from Egypt. Above them in the clouds there was someone whom she believed to be God the Father, his face in his hands. She then heard the Lady say: "And Yahweh is ashamed of his people." Then she saw Cain and Abel. As she wrote in her diary: "Near them on the ground in front of me, the jawbone of an ass. Suddenly Cain flees."

On another occasion, there was a loud cry: *"Babylon!"* And once during Holy Mass, she distinctly heard the word *"Ishmael"*, which was pronounced as *"Jishmael." "Ninevah, Ninevah, Ninevah!"* was also heard another time. Sometime later on, before going to bed one night, she heard the word *"Ephraim."* As she herself said: "I heard that call again but now on a higher and drawn out pitch. After that I could no longer get to sleep and I thought: 'What does it mean? I have never heard that word before.'" *"Lamech, Lamech, Lamech"* was another name called. On one occasion she also heard a voice moaning at intervals as many as seven times: *"Hagar-Hagar-Hagar-Hagar-Hagar-Hagar-Hagar."* Likewise, one day after receiving Holy Communion, a voice in a lamenting tone cried: *"Ahab! Ahab!"* I have written about all these biblical places and people in chapters 4 and 5.

Over the years the Lady appeared to Ida many times, always in the same way, bringing her messages which were recited very slowly and which her sister accurately recorded. Five years after the first apparition, on November 1, 1950, the dogma of the Assumption of the Blessed Virgin Mary was proclaimed by Pope Pius XII. It was only after this, on November 16, 1950, that her new title of *Lady or Mother of all Nations* was mentioned for the first time. This title is closely linked to the new dogma which she requested.

She said to Ida: "Now the moment has come for you to speak about Mary as *Co-Redemptrix, Mediatrix and Advocate under the title of the Lady of all Nations."* She later added: "It may be asked why this title is not mentioned in the messages of the first five years. It is because the dogma of the Assumption had to come first. All the dogmas which had preceded it concerned the life and the departure from this life of the Lady. The last and greatest Marian dogma will follow it."

Three months later, the date was February 11, 1951. It was the anniversary of the first day she appeared to Bernadette Soubirous in Lourdes where she said: "I am the Immaculate Conception." It was on that day in 1951 that she gave her prayer to the world. She said to Ida: *"I am the Lady, Mary, Mother of all Nations. You may say 'the Lady of all Nations' or 'Mother of all Nations,' who once was Mary.* I have come precisely on this day to tell you that I wish to be known as this. Tell all the children of men, the children of all the countries in the world, that they must be *one!"* Then she said: "All men must return to the Cross; and only then, will peace and tranquility reign. Repeat after me this prayer in front of the Cross. It is a trinitarian prayer:

> *"**Lord Jesus Christ**, Son of the **Father**, send now Your **Spirit** over the earth. Let the Holy Spirit live in the hearts of all nations, that they may be preserved from degeneration, disaster and war. May the Lady of all Nations, who once was Mary, be our Advocate. Amen."*

She continued: "My child, this prayer is so short and simple that everyone can say it in his own language before his own crucifix, and those who have no crucifix can repeat it to themselves. This is the message which I have come to give to you today for I have now to come to tell you that I want to save souls. Everybody should collaborate in this great work...."

Ida described how she recited the prayer to her: "Suddenly I noticed that the Lady was becoming even more beautiful than she already was. The light which always surrounded her became much brighter and sharper so that I could hardly bear to look at it. She raised her hands which were normally turned downwards, and joined them. Her face became so heavenly, so sublime, that one simply cannot express it in words. Her figure grew even more translucent and surpassingly beautiful. I stayed looking at her in rapture and wondered what would happen next. Then the Lady began to recite the prayer: '*Lord Jesus Christ, Son of the Father ...*' O, the way in which she said this! Never before did I hear anyone pray like this ... '*Send now Your Spirit,*' she said, stressing the '*now*'. '*Let the Holy Spirit live in the hearts of all nations,*' she continued, this time stressing the '*all*'. She also pronounced the word '*Amen*' so solemnly. No one could pray the way she did, so beautifully, so impressively."

At first, the words *"who once was Mary"* caused considerable surprise, even bewilderment. As Ida herself confessed: "I must admit that the words '*who once was Mary*' were very strange indeed. I said to myself but surely you always are Mary. Afterwards, when I passed on the prayer to Fr. Frehe, he said: 'What on earth is this '*who once was Mary*?' She can't have said this. She is and would always be Mary.' 'I do not know what it means,' I said, 'but I have got to pass it on faithfully just as she said it.'"

Indeed, when the text of the prayer was submitted to the ecclesiastical authorities for approval, they too made it quite clear that they had objections to those words. This explains why when the prayer was first printed the words *"who once was Mary"* were omitted. But the Lady did not approve of this omission: "No change must be made in the text of the prayer," she said to Ida. "The words '*who once was Mary*' must remain. Tell the theologians that I am not satisfied with the change in the prayer. '*May the Lady of all*

Nations, who once was Mary, be our Advocate' must remain." Eventually the complete text of the prayer was approved and the Lady later said to Ida: "Tell your bishop that I am satisfied. The text of the prayer is now correct."

On March 1, 1951, she appeared again to Ida and said: "See my image. Look at it well. Keep all of this in your memory. See, I am standing on the globe. My two feet are solidly planted upon it. You can clearly distinguish my hands, my face, my hair, and my veil, but all the rest is hazy. Take a good look at what protrudes above my head and from each side at the height of my shoulders." Ida responded: "It is a Cross. I could see the horizontal arms tipping out on each side and, above your head, the upright arm." Then the scene unfolded with the Lady removing her sash and demonstrating to Ida how she bound it around her: first a complete turn, then another. "Listen and remember what this signifies," she said. "This betokens the loin-cloth of my Son (on the Cross)."

The Lady then said: "You would have a picture made of this. You would propagate it at the same time as the prayer which I gave you. Such is my wish today. The prayer is to be translated in various languages. My child, I emphasize that all of this must be done. I am going to tell you why I present myself in this way. I am the Lady standing in front of the Cross. The head, the hands, the feet are similar to those of man but the rest of the body bears evidence to the Spirit. The Son came by the will of the Father, and now it is the Spirit who must come into the world." Then, tracing with a movement of her hand a semi-circle above her head from one arm of the Cross to the other, she showed an arc of a very special type of light in which were written words formed of black letters. From the left, "The Lady"; on the top "of all" and to the right, the word "nations." She said: "Never has the world known such times or such a decline in faith. I wish to be the Lady of all Nations. Not of one nation, but of *all* nations...."

She appeared in front of the Cross standing on the globe with her feet resting on the top of Europe. "The Low Countries (the Netherlands) are on the verge of corruption," she lamented, "and that is exactly why I have placed my foot upon the Low Countries. Yet it is from these Low Countries that my prayer would spread all over the world. Look where I am placing my feet. One is on Germany, the other on the Low Countries. 'Poor people of Germany! Have you not yet learnt your lesson? Christians of Germany, return to the Cross. The people of the Low Countries have likewise embarked upon the wrong path.'"

Around the globe were numerous sheep, both white and black. Many of the sheep are depicted looking up to the Cross. In other words, they were looking up at the Lamb crucified on the Cross; he who was the shepherd of the flock but was at the same time both priest and victim! The Ewe, the mother of the Lamb, was standing in front of the Cross. As she said to Ida: "The flock of sheep symbolizes the nations of the entire world who will not find rest except in lying down and peacefully contemplating the Cross, the central point of this world."

Ida then saw in the middle of each of the Virgin's hands what looked like a scar of a wound emitting three rays which appeared to shine on the sheep below. She smiled and said: "These three rays are those of grace, of redemption, of peace. By the grace of my Lord and Master, the Father, in his love for humanity, sent upon the earth his only Son, the Redeemer. Both now wish to send the Holy and True Spirit. He alone can bring peace. So, grace, redemption, peace. However, in this era the Father and the Son wish to send Mary, the Lady of all Nations, as Co-Redemptrix, Mediatrix and Advocate. Now I have given a clear explanation of the image. You, my child, are the instrument destined to transmit these things. Take good care that the prayer (it is short and powerful) be spread as speedily as possible. The picture would go from *nation to nation* and city to city. Act promptly and use modern methods."

Indeed, the propagation of the prayer, which was given enthusiastic approval in the Netherlands in 1951, developed into a worldwide movement in a short time. With the approbation of more than sixty bishops abroad, the prayer and the picture have found their way into millions of copies, in over sixty languages, and into the farthest corners of the earth. Without any sort of publicity, requests for it were pouring and are still pouring in every day as the Lady had prophesied: "You will find that the prayer would spread on its own accord. In the same manner that snow flakes flutter about and fall upon the earth covering it with a thick blanket, so too would my prayer and the picture which now circulates throughout the world, spread into the hearts of all nations."

The task of painting the picture was entrusted to the German painter Heinrich Repke. Ida gave an account of it in her diary: "Time and time again I had to explain to the painter what the Lady was like. Of course, this was terribly difficult. I tried to explain to him as well as possible. However, the painter had an almost impossible job to do, especially painting the expression of her face, her eyes, her hands, the rays of light from her hands, the light surrounding her, and her translucent form. In the end I asked the Lady whether the picture had her approval, but she just smiled. I then told the painter: 'It is alright as it is. Do not do anything further to it.' In my opinion it is altogether impossible to picture Mary or to make a likeness of her as I saw her."

This reminds me of the painting of Jesus as the Divine Mercy. When Sr. Faustina Kowalska was dissatisfied with the painter's portrayal of his face, she wept in disappointment and complained to Jesus: "Who would paint you as beautiful as you are?" In answer Jesus said to her: "Not in the beauty of the color, nor of the brush lies the greatness of this image, but in my graces."

On April 29, 1951, the Blessed Virgin revealed: "The new dogma will be the dogma of the Co-Redemptrix. I emphasize 'Co.' I have already said how much controversy this dogma would arouse. The Church of Rome will have a long struggle over it, but will finally proclaim it. I have said that these times are our times. Here is what this means. The world is in a state of corruption. It is becoming more and more superficial. It no longer knows where it is going. It is because of this that the Father has sent me in the capacity of Advocate in order to announce the coming of the **Holy Spirit**. The world will not be saved through violence. The world will be saved by the **Spirit**. *The image and its dissemination — this is the work prerequisite to the dogma.* Later, this image would be the emblem of the Co-Redemptrix. The Lady, the Mother, has suffered the sufferings of the Son, both spiritual and corporal."

And how she suffered! In fact, it is my interpretation that a vision which the Lady showed to Ida on January 3, 1946, was meant to symbolize a type of Mary. Ida recorded the vision in her diary: "Someone unexpectantly arrives. She is on horseback and clad in a breastplate. I asked: 'Who is this?' and I hear: 'Joan of Arc.' " This is the young girl who led and fought at the head of the French army and saved France from her enemy. In the end she suffered excruciatingly by being burnt at the stake. Mary, on the other hand, was on a much greater mission. She cooperated with her Son the Redeemer in saving, not only France, but the whole world from her enemy Satan. It called for a much, much greater suffering! Like Joan of Arc, she is leading the battle in the final stages of this conflict with Satan and his seed, which began in the Garden of Eden (Genesis 3:15).

On July 2, 1951, she said to Ida: "Now, look and listen. What I am going to say is an explanation of the new dogma. I am standing on the globe in front of the Cross of the Redeemer in the capacity of Co-Redemptrix, Mediatrix and Advocate. By the will of the Father, the Redeemer came into the world. For that, the Father had recourse to the Lady. From the Lady, and from her alone — I stress the word, alone — the Redeemer took flesh and blood; that is to say, his body. From my Lord and Master, the Redeemer received his divinity. In this way the Lady became the Co-Redemptrix by the *will* of the Father. It was necessary to begin with the dogma of the Assumption. Then the last and greatest would follow. Mankind has been entrusted to the Mother. That was when the Son said: 'Woman, behold your Son,' and to John: 'Behold your mother.' Tell that to your theologians. I do not come to bring any new doctrine. The doctrine already exists. Say this to your theologians: 'Already, from the beginning, she was Co-Redemptrix.' "

Now, the Blessed Virgin emphasized the prefix "Co." It comes from the Latin word "cum" (also col-, com-, cor-). And so, in referring to Mary, it is not intended to mean "co-equal," but "cooperating with" and "companion of" the Redeemer in a supportive role but also completely subjugated to him. This, of course, is very unlike the second verse in the well-known Eucharistic hymn the *Tantum Ergo,* composed by St. Thomas Aquinas: "Glory be to God the Father. Praise to his co-equal Son." In short, "Co-Redemptrix" does not mean "Co-equal Redemptrix." The co-pilot, for example, is not equal to the pilot!

There is in addition this major difference between the two. God could have redeemed the world by himself and could have appeared on earth as Adam did — without a mother. But he chose otherwise. He chose to be made man through a woman. On the other hand, the Co-Redemptrix, his mother, Mary, could never, never have redeemed the world on her own. She was only the companion of the Redeemer just as the first Eve, as the Bible says, was the "companion" of the first Adam (Genesis 3:12). It was a woman and a man who sinned in the Garden of Eden, and in God's inscrutable, logical and providential plan, it therefore had to be a man *and* a woman to redeem the world. It is as simple as that. Everyone should also be able to understand this. It does not call for any theological sense. Common sense will do!

She continued speaking to Ida: "From the beginning the handmaid of the Lord was chosen to be Co-Redemptrix. Tell your theologians that they can find this in their books and that you are not bringing a new doctrine. Tell the theologians I would see to its realization. This is why the Lady of all Nations has been compelled to come now, in these present times, for she is the Immaculate Conception, *and as a consequence of this,* the Co-Redemptrix, Mediatrix and Advocate. These three are but one. Is that clearly understood, theologians?"

But this has been "clearly understood" by many of us since 1830 when she appeared to St. Catherine Labouré in the Rue du Bac in Paris and showed her the Miraculous Medal. In this medal are all the symbols that Mary is the Co-Redemptrix, Mediatrix and Advocate. Indeed, the "M" under the Cross is as much for "Mother" as it is for "Mary." But its true name is not the Miraculous Medal. It was originally called the Medal of the Immaculate Conception!

On another occasion she explained: "It was with the departure of the Lord Jesus Christ, and only then, that the Lady became Mediatrix and Advocate. It was with the departure of the Lord Jesus Christ that he made a gift to the nations of the Lady of all Nations. Never has Mary officially been called Co-Redemptrix. Never has she officially been called Mediatrix. Never has she officially been called Advocate. These three functions form one whole. It would constitute the keystone of Marian doctrines."

On the fiftieth apparition, on May 31, 1954, she said: "I have chosen this day because on this day the Lady will receive what would later be her coronation. Theologians, and you apostles of the Lord Jesus Christ, I have given you the justification of the dogma, work then for this dogma. This is the date when the Co-Redemptrix, Mediatrix and Advocate would receive her title, duly proclaimed, of the Mother of all Nations." Indeed, on May 31, 1996, the public veneration of the Mother of God under the title the Lady or Mother of all Nations was officially approved by the two bishops of Haarlem (Netherlands), Bishop Hendrik Bomers and his Assistant Bishop Mgr. Josef Punt. Her prophecy of May 31, 1954 was thus fulfilled!

May 31 is a very historic date. It is also the last day in the month dedicated to Mary. Interestingly, the Church also once celebrated the feast of Mary, Mediatrix of all graces, on May 31, and later on it became the feast of Mary, Queen of the Universe. Today, May 31 is the feast of the Visitation.

She also warned: "You apostles, you nations, fall upon your knees before your Lord and Creator. Express your gratitude. The science of the world has turned men away from gratitude. They no longer know their Creator. So you nations, be warned. Bow down before your Creator. My child, do you realize what times you are living in? Never in its history has the world experienced a time like the present one — such a decline in faith."

Then on another occasion she warned: "The enemy of the Lord Jesus Christ has done his work slowly but persistently. The posts are manned. His preparations are nearly finished. Nations, be warned! The spirit of lies and deceit is seducing many. It won't be long before the breaking of the storm. Great evils threaten the world. The Churches would be undermined even further. Please realize why I come as the Lady of all Nations. I come to assemble all nations in the Spirit, the Spirit of Truth, the Holy Spirit.... The sheep must be gathered together into one flock, one great community." She also said in Amsterdam: *It would be known that I am the Lady of all Nations when the great powers crumble and political and economic conflicts break out...."*

Now, she was seen in front of the Cross with her hair loose and falling down beyond her shoulders. In other words, she "let her hair down," literally and figuratively. This "hairdo" fascinated me. And then I found out that there was a possible biblical significance to this. In the Book of Judges there is the "Song of Deborah," which was sung to celebrate the great victory of the army of the Israelites over the powerful pagan army of Sisera. The song describes the hairstyle of the Israelites: "That the warriors in Israel unbound their hair, that the people came forward with a will, for this bless Yahweh!" (Judges 5:1-2). According to the Jerusalem Bible, this was a well-known custom in battle and it is said that the modern Bedouin still observe this ritual of war. And so, she appeared in "battle array" (Song 6:10) in front of the Cross, threw down the gauntlet to her enemy, and called for the dogma which would officially recognize her victory over Satan as Co-Redemptrix and as promised in Genesis 3:15.

Another apparition in which she wore a similar hairstyle in recent times was in Garabandal when she appeared as Our Lady of Mount Carmel. Mount Carmel was the site of the great battle between Elijah and the pagan worshippers of Baal during the reign of King Ahab when Elijah called down fire from heaven and won the battle. Israel then returned to the worship of the one true God.

She first appeared in Amsterdam on March 25, 1945, the feast of the Annunciation. In Garabandal her first apparition was on July 2, 1961, which at that time was the feast of the Visitation. Her next major apparition was in Medjugorje on June 24, 1981, the feast of John the Baptist. The logic of this time sequence of apparitions suddenly unfolded itself to me. Firstly, it was the Annunciation, then the Visitation, and then the birth of John the Baptist, who prepared the way for the Second Coming of her Son. It was a true biblical sequence.

Nine months after the Annunciation, she gave birth to the Prince of Peace, and thereby became the Queen of Peace. It is under this title that she appears in Medjugorje in Yugoslavia. As Sr. Lucia of Fatima once said, the peace of the world has been entrusted to her. But her children, the nations, are at war. When in 1917, at the height of World War I, Pope Benedict XV urged the Catholic world to implore Our Lady to intercede with her Divine Son for the gift of peace, the Blessed Virgin responded just eight days later by appearing in Fatima as the Lady of the Rosary with a white chaplet in her hand. It was her spiritual and most powerful weapon. It was her answer to war. World War I ended on November 11, 1918. Significantly, it was the feast of St. Martin of Tours, who is the patron saint of soldiers. How appropriate! World War II ended on August 15, 1945. It was the feast of the Assumption of the Blessed Virgin Mary. And so, she spends her heaven doing good on earth for her children.

She is truly the Queen of Peace. During World War II the United States entered the war on December 8, 1942. It was an entry which won the day for the Allies. It was the feast of the Immaculate Conception. Six years after the surrender of Japan on August 15, 1945, Japan signed another formal pact in San Francisco pertaining to its surrender. It was called the Second World War Peace Treaty. It was on September 8, 1951, the feast of the Nativity of the Blessed Virgin Mary. The signing of the Intermediate Range Nuclear Forces Treaty in Washington by Mikhail Gorbachev and Ronald Reagan, abolishing medium range missiles in Europe, took place on December 8, 1987, the feast of the Immaculate Conception. The Communist Party in Russia suddenly and dramatically collapsed on August 22, 1991. It was the feast of the Queenship of Mary!

But the apparitions of the Lady of all Nations (as she now wishes to be called in this era) in Lourdes, Fatima, Garabandal and Akita were all associated with the Eucharist. In Amsterdam, the first of several Eucharistic experiences that Ida had was in 1958, when she saw a bright Host, which she said was "like fire." When I first visited Ida at her home in 1992, it was on July 17. As she greeted me in her doorway, she exclaimed: "Do you know that this is the anniversary of the miracle of the Host?" At that time I did not. But it was not the first Eucharistic miracle in Amsterdam. The first one occurred in 1345!

Six weeks previously she had said to Ida on May 31, 1957: "Before the Lord Jesus Christ ascended to the Father he gave you the great mystery, the miracle of every day, every minute. He gave you himself. No, nations (she shook her head vehemently as she said this), not merely a remembrance; no, nations, listen to what he said: not just an idea, but himself, under the appearance of a little piece of bread, under the appearance of wine. This is how the Lord wants to come among you day after day. Do accept it. He gives you the foretaste — the foretaste of eternal life." And so, it is the Eucharist and the Rosary. It is the dream of two pillars seen by Don Bosco in 1862. They are the passports to peace and harmony on earth. They are the weapons to defeat the powers of darkness.

This then brings to an end my research on the *Lady, Mary, Mother of all Nations*. It stemmed from my firm belief in the authenticity of the messages of the Blessed Virgin Mary given to us through Ida Peerdeman in Amsterdam. They are the urgent cries of a loving mother warning her children of an impending disaster, one which will be worse than the flood. Undoubtedly, the threat of another and greater nuclear holocaust hangs over our heads like a sword of Damocles, but *homo sapiens sapiens* has the ability, unique in the animal kingdom, to learn from the experiences of history. However, I sometimes wonder how sapient we are! This is because apparently there is one thing that can be said about history and it is that man learns nothing from history. The "flood" is history. The "fire next time" may well be history's second major global catastrophe, if we do not convert and stop offending God.

After Hiroshima and Nagasaki a generation has grown to adulthood in full awareness of the horrific destruction that nuclear weapons can unleash upon mankind. The knowledge of what fission and fusion of the atom can do has now become part of the historical legacy of mankind, but whether we choose to learn from that legacy or not is up to us. Albert Einstein once said: "The unleashed power of the atom has changed everything save our modes of thinking, and we thus drift towards unparalleled catastrophe. Our defence is not in armaments, nor in science, nor in going underground. Our defence is in law and order." And on another occasion, this great scientist said: "As long as there are sovereign nations possessing great power, war is inevitable. I do not believe that civilization would be wiped out in a war fought with the atomic bomb. Perhaps two thirds of the people of the earth might be killed. But enough men capable of thinking, and enough books, would be left to start again and civilization could be restored."

But there is hope. All these threats can be averted if we do as our Mother says. Happily, she has promised that in the end all will be *one* and that her Immaculate Heart will triumph. When the dogma, the last dogma in Marian history, is proclaimed it would be her crowning glory. Then, as she said, "the Lady of all Nations would give peace, true peace, to the world, and more than ever before, all generations will call me blessed."

With her "Yes" at the Annunciation, she immediately became the *Mother of God.* It was her first title and eventually the first Marian dogma. It was the birth of the most romantic religion of man. It was the "beginning" of redemption. It was "finished" on Calvary on that Friday that we call "Good." It was there and then that she became the *Mother of all Nations.* It was the last will and testament of the Redeemer as she stood in front of the Cross when he was speaking to John. It is fitting therefore that this title should be linked to the proposed final Marian dogma, *Mary, Co-Redemptrix, Advocate and Mediatrix.*

"Abba, Father!" we say, and so, the day will soon come when all her children will call her "Imma, Mother." In anticipation of this, I say to all of us, let her prayer resound from pole to pole, from nation to nation:

> *"Lord Jesus Christ, Son of the Father, send now Your Spirit over the earth. Let the Holy Spirit live in the hearts of all nations, that they may be preserved from degeneration, disaster and war. May the Lady of all Nations, who once was Mary, be our Advocate. Amen."*